"Dennis Edwards has written the true 'Christianity of Ch
this book's introduction—a Christianity that for four hundred years has stood in deep contrast to the 'Christianity of this land.' The difference between the two is stark, and we are at a moment in history which will determine if a new generation of white Christians are ready to join the leadership of black Christians to change that. Until white Christianity welcomes the leadership of black and brown pastors and leaders, that conversion to the Christ of the Gospels will not come. Edwards shows us that it is believers from marginalized groups who have the power to transform American Christianity."

—**JIM WALLIS**, president of Sojourners, editor-in-chief of *Sojourners* magazine, and author of *America's Original Sin*

"American Christianity is warped, sick from racial injustice. But the power of the gospel is real, and Dennis Edwards shows us in wonderful prose and detail that God's power resides in the marginalized. They have the Holy Ghost power to bring the sick back to health and revive the church. Highly recommended!"

—**MICHAEL O. EMERSON**, professor of sociology at the University of Illinois at Chicago and author of *Divided by Faith* and *Transcending Racial Barriers*

"Dennis Edwards calls our attention to the margins where, for generations, faithful Christians have followed and proclaimed Jesus. Steeped in hard-earned wisdom and keen biblical insight, *Might from the Margins* envisions a Christianity that trades the destructive power of racial whiteness for solidarity with women and men of color who have long known the life-giving power of God. It's an urgent and gracious call, one that every Christian would do well to heed."

—**DAVID W. SWANSON**, pastor and author of *Rediscipling the White Church*

"In *Might from the Margins*, Dennis Edwards models both a priestly and prophetic witness in one seamless voice as he unveils the forces of evil and oppression that have distorted white American evangelicalism for too long. If you are looking for someone with integrity to point you toward Jesus-shaped solidarity and through the maze of racial oppression and abusive power dynamics, moving toward our ultimate hope in God's new world, then read this book. It is a compelling vision forward, grounded in Scripture and God's delivering presence for those with their 'backs against the wall.'"

—**DREW G. I. HART**, assistant professor of theology at Messiah University and author of *Who Will Be a Witness? Igniting Activism for God's Justice, Love, and Deliverance*

"*Might from the Margins* is brilliant; teased out from the pages of Scripture and insightful sociocultural analysis. It is thoughtful; perceptively getting to the heart of issues with depth and care. It is prophetic; refusing to give sway to the forces of injustice and supremacy that seek to silence often unattended-to voices. And it is pastoral; written with a pastor's heart for people long trod upon by those claiming to be friend and sibling in Christ. It is also humbling, as is every interaction I have with my mentor, Dennis Edwards, who patiently helps me better identify my own, and my fellow white folks', blind spots and indifferent acts of aggression and antagonism toward communities pushed to the margins of a society shaped by and centered on whiteness and its derivative injustices. I'm thankful for a book that deals with power in a unique, creative, and compelling way. May the church see something of a deeper collective fruitfulness because of it!"

—**ADAM L. GUSTINE**, assistant director of social concerns seminars at the University of Notre Dame Center for Social Concerns and author of *Becoming a Just Church*

"The apostle Paul tells the Corinthians that God chose the marginalized, the 'nobodies,' to rob the elite and popular, the 'somebodies,' of their status (1 Corinthians 1:28). That is what *Might from the Margins* is all about. Dennis Edwards highlights how the gospel is God's power to lift up every valley and make low every mountain. Some readers will find this book troubling and upsetting, others will be filled with hope and courage. What a bold, beautiful, and incisive message for a church that God wants to transform!"

—**NIJAY GUPTA**, associate professor of New Testament at Portland Seminary

MIGHT
from the
MARGINS

MIGHT
from the
MARGINS

The GOSPEL'S POWER to TURN the TABLES on INJUSTICE

Dennis R. Edwards

✝ERALD
PRESS

Harrisonburg, Virginia

Herald Press
PO Box 866, Harrisonburg, Virginia 22803
www.HeraldPress.com

Library of Congress Cataloging-in-Publication Data
Names: Edwards, Dennis R. (Biblical scholar), author.
Title: Might from the margins : the gospel's power to turn the tables on injustice / Dennis R. Edwards.
Description: Harrisonburg, Virginia : Herald Press, 2020. | Includes bibliographical references.
Identifiers: LCCN 2020011640 (print) | LCCN 2020011641 (ebook) | ISBN 9781513806013 (paperback) | ISBN 9781513806020 (hardcover) | ISBN 9781513806037 (ebook)
Subjects: LCSH: Church and minorities.
Classification: LCC BV639.M56 E39 2020 (print) | LCC BV639.M56 (ebook) | DDC 261.8—dc23
LC record available at https://lccn.loc.gov/2020011640
LC ebook record available at https://lccn.loc.gov/2020011641

Study guides are available for many Herald Press titles at www.HeraldPress.com.

MIGHT FROM THE MARGINS
© 2020 by Herald Press, Harrisonburg, Virginia 22803. 800-245-7894.
All rights reserved.
Library of Congress Control Number: 2020011640
International Standard Book Number: 978-1-5138-0601-3 (paperback); 978-1-5138-0603-7 (ebook)
Printed in United States of America
Cover and interior design by Merrill Miller

Unless otherwise noted, Scripture text is quoted, with permission, from the *New Revised Standard Version*, © 1989, Division of Christian Education of the National Council of Churches of Christ in the United States of America.

Scripture quotations marked (NIV) are taken from the *Holy Bible, New International Version*®, NIV®. Copyright © 1973, 1978, 1984, 2011 by Biblica, Inc.™ Used by permission of Zondervan. All rights reserved worldwide. www .zondervan.com The "NIV" and "New International Version" are trademarks registered in the United States Patent and Trademark Office by Biblica, Inc.™

24 23 22 21 20   10 9 8 7 6 5 4 3 2 1

To grandsons Mays, August, Moses, and Asa:
May God use you to show the gospel's power
to turn the tables on injustice.

Contents

Foreword

I FOUNDED The Expectations Project in 2012 after working in public education as a teacher, researcher, teacher trainer, and policy analyst. I had come to believe that we will never eliminate the massive disparity in educational outcomes unless we advocate for systemic policy change, speak truth to power, and hold elected officials accountable.

As a Christian, I view faith communities as an important vehicle for that advocacy. Education equity is ultimately connected to deep belief that all children have unlimited potential because they are made in God's image and likeness. The God we serve doesn't believe that only white or wealthy kids are smart enough to achieve in school. Yet this disparity is often reflected in American public schools, so people of faith should advocate to change the system to better illustrate God's promises.

Eight years ago, as a newly minted founder, I had a grand vision to deeply engage my white evangelical Christian brothers and sisters in our work. I was buoyed by the recent inroads in social justice issues like climate change and immigration reform. White evangelicals' large numbers and proximity to power were significant and, honestly, intoxicating. I was confident that with the right strategies and the right allies, we could build an interracial faithful coalition that could bring educational equity and systemic change to American public schools.

The work was never easy, to be clear. It felt like we were dragging some white communities along with us, kicking and screaming. We had to get creative to get their attention, as education inequality is unfamiliar to many white faith communities. It simply isn't in their backyard like it is for most Black and brown communities. Also, I didn't want to be in the business of racial reconciliation. That is definitely someone else's wonderful mission and calling; it was never mine. But those interracial conversations required it. And it was painfully exhausting.

And then 2016 happened. As a Black Christian woman, I struggled to comprehend how nearly 80 percent of my white evangelical Christian brothers and sisters voted for a presidential candidate that, at best, trafficked in dangerous racial tropes and hurtful stereotypes. The very nature of our organization's work centers around the racial history and institutional discrimination that is intertwined in education inequality. How could I possibly reconcile this newly revealed white evangelical reality in the context of our mission?

As I grieved for our nation and the church, I did some uncomfortable self-reflection. Why had I always felt the need to have white Christians take a significant role in improving our nation's public schools? Did I think we couldn't do it without them? Were the voices and power of Black and brown faith leaders not enough? After all, who is better able to determine what is needed in our communities than us? I'd subconsciously internalized the idea that white Christians were essential to the work of "saving" Black schools.

Ironically, I grew up in Detroit, where our family attended a large and influential Black church in the city. Like many in the Black church tradition, my congregation did not shy away from political action. I was raised on Black church advocacy and action—seeing Black pastors hold elected officials accountable for community change. But somewhere along the way, I'd lost hold of that central belief and truth: we have power all by ourselves. And we can be enough.

Dennis Edwards's book, *Might from the Margins*, lays out a much-needed theological framework that both explores and celebrates the power of marginalized communities. By leaning into the wisdom of our Black Christian ancestors, he deftly examines the inherently strong voice, knowledge, and proximity that we bring to bear on the challenges in our own neighborhoods. And perhaps most importantly, he gives space to and validates the frustration that many Christians of color feel at this moment. Dennis lays out the challenges we face plainly and offers a place to look for solutions. And he does all of this with a tough love and call to action that the body of Christ and white American evangelicals desperately need.

As for me and my organization's work? The Expectations Project will always welcome our white evangelical allies and co-conspirators to join us at the table. But our education advocacy table is set by, centered around, and led by Black and brown faith communities. So come and break bread. Just remember to feast quietly while you learn from us and while you follow us. I believe *Might from the Margins* provides an excellent road map for the journey.

—Nicole Baker Fulgham,
founder and president of The Expectations Project

Introduction

SHOOT ME IF I EVER work for white evangelicals again!" I said those words to Susan, my wife, around the time I finished six years of pastoral ministry at an overwhelmingly white church in Washington, DC. We were indeed in Washington, DC, and not a suburb within Virginia or Maryland, whose residents often claim DC as home. Most of the prominent members of that DC church lived outside the city, even though the church gathered within the city. The District of Columbia has the nickname Chocolate City and is where several of my paternal and maternal forebears lived for decades after slavery. My experiences at that church were part of many interactions among a cross section of Christians in the USA that revealed distortions regarding power.[1]

This book serves to affirm the power that apparently powerless people possess. The power of marginalized people is frequently overlooked by the dominant culture. Even so, we who have been in the shadows have power to reshape American

Christianity. Part of reshaping Christianity is telling the truth about how we understand and perform the gospel of Jesus Christ. My elders would say, "Tell the truth and shame the devil!" My desire is to tell the truth from Scripture and from experience. I hope to blow some wind into the sails of faithful people of color who are fighting against injustice. As a biblical scholar, I dig into the Scripture text throughout this book. And as a pastor, I reflect on human interactions and contemporary matters. Much of the motivation for writing this book came from my pastoral experiences, including the ones that prompted me to make that proclamation of frustration to my wife.

EXPERIENCE AS TEACHER

Since I've served God's people in churches and Christian educational institutions for over thirty years, I have plenty of stories. Some of them reveal the way that white Christianity minimizes people of color. Some of my stories are benign, compared to those of friends of mine, but I don't intend to create a competition for who has the worst stories of white Christianity's treatment of marginalized people. I will, however, begin by giving an account of a meeting that continually serves as a paradigm for me of interracial interactions. My hope is that you can relate and understand more of why I wrote this book.

One of the innumerable, frustrating, racially insensitive meetings I had with church people took place in the fellowship hall of the church where I had recently been called to serve. That predominately white church, with its extremely well-educated attendees, had a slogan posted in the bulletin as well as on the sign in front of the building: "A church for all peoples." The church attendees' level of education and their self-description highlight the irony of that meeting in the fellowship hall.

Parents of teenagers and church leadership gathered at the request of young adults who volunteered as youth leaders. These youth leaders came with an ultimatum: They would no longer lead the youth group if it included *neighborhood kids*. They wanted a group for just *our kids*.

At that point in the church's life, most of the families with children lived outside DC, either in the Maryland or Virginia suburbs. Ironically, the kids who lived closest to the church building were the ones whose presence in the youth group was unwelcome. The church prided itself on having created and staffed an after-school program, largely for tutoring local DC students. Virtually all the children in the program were African American. Some of the children from this program, along with the offspring of church members, had formerly been part of a single youth group—until the night of that meeting.

The meeting might have ended quickly if I had not opened my mouth. All the parents—some of whom were church leaders —appeared content to leave the neighborhood kids out of the youth group. I raised my hand to say that I had a problem with this new development. I pointed out that my own children were *neighborhood kids*. I wanted the group to see that they were using *neighborhood kids* as a euphemism for *black kids*. Someone recognized my situation and acknowledged that my oldest son, who was about to be old enough for the group, could certainly be part of it! I argued that being the only black kid in the group would present its own unique set of challenges. My point was minimized when a mom in the group said it would be no different from her daughter being the only twelfth-grader when all the other kids were younger. I still scratch my head over her comment. Ironically, the church had recently adopted a mission statement that stressed reconciliation of people "across race, class, and culture," so I was finding the discussion troubling and inconsistent with our stated values. I was hoping that our senior pastor would raise his voice, creating a teachable moment to call us back to our mission, even if it meant finding new youth group leaders. But the senior pastor remained quiet throughout the evening.

I went on to stress that segregating the youth group was problematic and that a church must not turn kids away. My viewpoint gained no traction. The church leaders wanted the neighborhood kids to be part of the after-school program, but the youth group would be just for the offspring of church attendees along with the friends of those church families, none of whom lived in DC or were African American. Finally, in exasperation, I asked, "Well, if the youth are going to be separate, then at least can the groups be separate and equal?" I thought the phrase "separate and equal" would highlight the wrongheaded direction of the meeting. It did not. The young leaders and the white parents got what they wanted. I later requested that my job description be altered so I could be a pastoral presence for neighborhood kids who were not welcome to be part of the church's youth group.

One sad thing about my story of that meeting in the fellowship hall is how typical such experiences are in Christian circles. I don't just mean the confusion about the best way to minister to teenagers. What I mean is thinly veiled racism, communicated as a ministry strategy or evangelistic concern. Over the years I've personally known or have been aware of numerous people of color who got involved in white evangelical institutions, genuinely believing the organization wanted our input so that it could change for the better, but we got burned in the process. I realize not all white Christians are party to the racism of American Christianity. These followers of Jesus are often identified as allies in anti-racism and other justice efforts. Allies can be helpful. An African American Christian leader I know prefers the term *accomplice* rather than *ally*. His point is that while allies lend support, accomplices are willing to pay the same price that you pay. Despite the presence of white allies—or even accomplices—discussing racism and other aspects of injustice in majority white settings can be traumatic. It is painful to rehearse the realities of being marginalized in your own country, only to have your concerns and perspectives dismissed by white people.

CHRISTIAN WHITE FRAGILITY

In her book *White Fragility: Why It's So Hard for White People to Talk about Racism*, Robin DiAngelo, a white educator, addresses white people in an attempt to help them understand racism as well as their reluctance to discuss—much less dismantle—its power. DiAngelo describes the phenomenon of "aversive racism," which was operative in the church meeting I just described. DiAngelo writes, "Aversive racism is a manifestation of racism that well-intentioned people who see themselves as educated and progressive are more likely to exhibit. It exists under the surface of consciousness because it conflicts with consciously held beliefs of racial equality and justice. Aversive racism is a subtle but insidious form, as aversive racists enact racism in ways that allow them to maintain a positive self-image (e.g., 'I have lots of friends of color'; 'I judge people by the content of their character, not the color of their skin')."[2] According to DiAngelo, one of the ways that "white people enact racism while maintaining a positive self-image" is "avoiding direct racial language and using racially coded terms such as urban, underprivileged, diverse, sketchy, and good neighborhoods."[3]

The church in DC that I'd been called to serve certainly viewed itself as educated and progressive. In fact, a prominent member boasted more than once that there was an average of one graduate degree per person among the church attendees. When I applied for the associate pastor position, the search committee mailed me several pieces of information, including a description of the church. The last sentence of the one-page description stated that of the four hundred or so attendees, about 6 percent were African American; no other race or ethnic group was acknowledged or quantified. During my interview process, the search committee indicated that the church wanted that 6 percent statistic to increase, reflecting better connection to the neighborhood. I wasn't naive to the reality that my Ivy League degree and brown skin made me an attractive candidate for this congregation. I was given every reason to believe that the church desired more African Americans to attend. Yet the reality was that the church, like many others, "enacted racism while maintaining a positive self-image."[4]

Numerous books address the struggles of people of color. Some even illustrate and condemn white fragility. You surely have your own stories of how large portions of Christianity in the USA have been racist, sexist, bigoted, and generally toxic. I write as a pastor and biblical scholar, not a sociologist, and hope this book serves as another rallying point for us. Marginalized people are already changing the landscape of Christianity in the USA. This book is a biblical and pastoral affirmation of the power that the presumed powerless have to redefine Christianity in America. We don't just change the complexion of Christianity; we change its operation.

CENTERING PEOPLE OF COLOR

There is a scene in the blockbuster movie *Black Panther* where King T'Challa is incapacitated, and the kingdom of Wakanda is being threatened. The king's mother, Queen Ramonda, his sister, Shuri, Wakanda's agent Nakia, and CIA agent Everett Ross appear before M'Baku, the head of the Jabari Tribe, seeking their partnership. Agent Ross proceeds to explain the situation to M'Baku, who immediately begins to pound his staff on the ground and bark. Others of the Jabari instantly join in the barking until Agent Ross is drowned out and must stop talking. I was so thrilled by this scene that I nearly cheered and gave a standing ovation to the movie screen. That scene spoke to many people of color—especially African Americans—whose voices are muted by white people. We've suffered through *whitesplaining* and especially *whitemansplaining*. I've had white Christians tell me what it means to be black in America, attempting to regulate my viewpoints and behaviors in their presence. Agent Ross was an ally to the people of Wakanda, but he still needed to keep his mouth shut, listen, and learn.

Plenty of books challenge American Christians to behave justly. There are books that attempt to explain racism and the problem of whiteness. Oftentimes these books, including those written by people of color, are targeted at white Christians, especially evangelicals. Messages are aimed at the dominant culture with the hope that they'll change so that justice might trickle down. But justice must storm down like a waterfall, not trickle like a leaky faucet. Centering white people gives a subtle message that we are not able to exercise our own agency until we get white people's permission or buy-in. There's a sense in some circles that we need white people to *empower* us. Our voices seem to matter only if white people acknowledge us.

This book centers people of color. Perhaps the Agent Rosses of Christianity can listen and hold their tongues while we offer encouragement and challenge to each other.

While centering people of color, I do not dismiss the need for all people to work together in the service of the gospel. This book is not a covert attempt to guilt or shame white people. White people are not at the center of this book. My goal, however, is to join in the affirmation that marginalized people can lead in helping to make Christianity Jesus-like again. Distortions of the gospel are being used as wedges between people of different backgrounds. The nationalism among most white evangelicals can disfigure the face of Jesus revealed in the Scriptures. Jesus starts to look more like a white American than a Palestinian Jew of the first century. But not only might the image of Jesus be marred—so might the nature of the gospel itself. There are African Americans, for example, who are giving up on Christianity, and one of the ostensible reasons is the gospel enacted by white evangelicals.

IS THE GOSPEL GOOD NEWS FOR US?

One spring afternoon, my friend Bishop Gary Hayles sought me out to get my opinion about his conversations with a growing number of young men in his Cincinnati community. At first, a few young men approached Bishop Hayles to ask what it means to have faith in Jesus, and the bishop invited them to Starbucks to continue the conversation. The number of young men had been increasing over the weeks. The pressing issues for most of these young men (about twenty-five in number at the time I'm writing this) stem from their doubt, not of God, but about whether African Americans can be Christians in light of the way evangelicalism operates. They see how white evangelicals, by and large, are slow to denounce blatant racism, give unwavering support to President Trump, and also participate in the stereotyping and vilifying of non-white people, especially immigrants. I can relate to the concerns of these young men. These young men know that they are viewed as threats to the safety and well-being of many within white America. I also know what it feels like to be treated as if Christianity in the US has no room for me and to be perceived as threatening to white people.

During my years as a pastor at that church on Capitol Hill in Washington, DC, I would often cross paths with white people from my church, usually when walking between home and the Metro station or the nearby 7-Eleven store. I would smile and wave, but I noticed that instead of the church member offering a wave in return, their face would take on a fearful frown, their eyes would shift toward the ground, and their gait would quicken. Consequently, I developed a habit of identifying myself to white people who already knew me. I'd wave and call out, "It's Dennis!" Outside the church building I was simply another black man, not the pastor who looked them straight in the eye when serving them communion. I haven't yet shaken my habit of greeting white people. To this day I often say, "I'm Dennis," to white people who've already met me.

There was a recent spate of incidents of white people calling the police to investigate black people who were simply engaging in normal, day-to-day activities. One notable example is the 2018 arrest of two African American men who were sitting in a Philadelphia Starbucks, waiting for someone else to arrive, when a barista called the police. Dimensions of American society, such as housing, employment, and policing, have been structured around white people's fear of African Americans. As a result, African Americans are wary of the power of whiteness, a power that is at work among Christians too.

Bishop Hayles wanted my counsel regarding how to help these young men see that the Christianity that dehumanizes them does not represent the gospel of Jesus. These young men do not see Christianity as offering hope. Instead these young men are afraid. They fear that the faith of Bishop Hayles is complicit in the injustice they experience. In 1949, theologian, poet, and mystic Howard Thurman wrote *Jesus and the Disinherited*, a book that continues to speak prophetically to Christianity's failure to address power inequities. Thurman has an entire chapter on fear, and here he describes the fear that marginalized people have.

> In a society in which certain people or groups—by virtue of economic, social, or political power—have dead-weight advantages over others who are essentially without that kind of power, those who are thus disadvantaged know that they cannot fight back effectively, that they cannot protect themselves, and that they cannot demand protection from their persecutors. Any slight conflict, any alleged insult, any vague whim, any unrelated frustration, may bring down upon the head of the defenseless the full weight of naked physical violence.[5]

Keep in mind that Thurman wrote those words before the civil rights movement in the USA, but such fear is still alive among many immigrants as well as African Americans. Our fear, however, is not always of physical violence, although that fear can be present, and I sense it whenever I'm scrutinized by security officers in a department store or hear the sirens of a police car coming in my direction. People of color also fear being minimized, treated as ignorant, or generally dismissed as insignificant. Furthermore, white Christians often do little to assuage these fears. In fact, in many cases they are the source of the fear.

African Americans—men and women—often fear the police because of the history of brutality. The slogan and hashtag "Black lives matter" served to energize and mobilize many in the wake of several high-profile cases of police brutality. However, many white Christians are among those most offended by what may be seen as an innocuous slogan. Those three simple words are a cry for dignity, yet white Christians push back with "All lives matter," failing to recognize the fear that many of us have because of them. White Christians whose faith energizes their nationalism do not understand the type of power inherent in the gospel of Jesus Christ. The gospel of Jesus empowers. But the power of the gospel is not that of secular government. The gospel's power is not about social hierarchy. The gospel is the power of God for salvation. The gospel brings transformation. It creates witnesses who speak and act on behalf of Jesus. Systems energized through bullying bodies and suppressing spirits of fellow human beings—those who are also made in the image of God—do not portray the power of the gospel.

PROVOKING OUR POWER

By the grace of God, I have served in church ministry since 1987 and have also been an instructor of Bible at both the college and seminary levels. I write from the experience of many years of pastoral service and Scripture study. Those years have been exhilarating yet exhausting, draining yet instructive, delightful yet painful. Pastoral ministry is always challenging. It's well known that hurting people hurt people, and every pastor has countless stories of the pain caused by people who are

hurting. No church, despite its fervor, denominational affilia-
tion, or acts of community service, is inoculated against evil.
While Christians can claim salvation from sin, they can also
paradoxically be complicit in the devil's work. Christianity in
the USA has contributed to the racism, patriarchy, ableism, and
sexism of the broader society, diminishing people who are not
white, male, physically attractive, or able-bodied. Power is con-
centrated among white males. Consequently, millions of people are marginalized. The voices of a multitude are muted. The
body of Christ is distorted and misshapen because many parts
of that body are constricted for the sake of a powerful few.

In light of the toxicity of American Christianity, it's rea-
sonable to wonder now, as Howard Thurman did back in the
1940s, why African Americans, or anyone on the margins of
society, would become Christian. I believe that those who have
been marginalized have power that is not only unnoticed, but
often underutilized. We need to encourage each other to raise
our voices and bring all of who we are into Christian service.
We do not need to wait for permission or approval from the
dominant culture. Our power comes, first of all, from Jesus
Christ, whose gospel not only is about the life to come but also
affects life in the here and now.

ONE

The Power of God

For I am not ashamed of the gospel; it is the power of
God for salvation to everyone who has faith,
to the Jew first and also to the Greek.

—ROMANS 1:16

IT IS IMPOSSIBLE to count the vast number of analyses of the apostle Paul's letter to the Christians in Rome. Scholarly attention is primarily devoted to the words *gospel, salvation*, and *faith*—which not only appear in the verse quoted above but are ubiquitous throughout the apostle's writings. Right now, however, I want to focus on a seemingly less popular word from the above verse, one that is also frequent in Paul's letters: *everyone*. According to Romans 1:16, the gospel is power. The gospel is God's power, whose purpose is the salvation of everyone who believes. The apostle Paul may have had little idea of the size of the earth, and much less idea how many people populate the planet. Yet he believed that the story of Jesus Christ— the gospel—was power for salvation that every human could experience. In Romans, *everyone* refers to Jews and Gentiles (Greeks)—people from essentially different worlds. Paul makes explicit in Galatians that *everyone* means contrasting groups within society's social strata: "There is no longer Jew or Greek, there is no longer slave or free, there is no longer male and female; for all of you are one in Christ Jesus" (Galatians 3:28).

The gospel is an equalizer, dismantling the power distinctions erected by human systems. In the context of the USA, these words find resonance in the idealism of the Declaration of Independence, where Thomas Jefferson, in non-inclusive language typical of the time, declared that all men are created equal. It's ironic that a country espousing such lofty ideals is also a nation built on exploiting people of color—Indigenous peoples as well as others of non-European descent. My concern, however, does not start with government policy, per se, but with the way Christians in the USA have demonstrated the power of the gospel. To a large degree, white Christians have been the least willing to accept the teachings of the New Testament regarding the way the gospel empowers all people. To put it bluntly, white Christians generally operate in ways to protect their worldly self-interests, even at the expense of devaluing other human beings. This is especially evident in a large segment of Christianity in the USA—evangelicalism and fundamentalism. White evangelicals have created space to construct and defend unjust systems, often fortified by the way they define the gospel.

When the gospel is defined as belief in propositions about Jesus in order to validate an individual's personal relationship with God and acquire eternal life, the value given to other human beings is a secondary or tertiary matter, or perhaps does not even exist among an individual believer's list of concerns.

However, there is a movement among many Christians to re-capture the New Testament's presentation of the gospel. The gospel empowers others, and that power is often most visible among those who have been least respected, including the physically challenged, people with dark skin, women, and people who have been displaced from their homeland. I am among those who desire the church to preach, teach, and demonstrate a more robust gospel. That robust gospel includes at least these ideas:

- The gospel is the story of Jesus.
- The gospel includes the teachings and actions of Jesus.
- The gospel includes liberation from sin through the death and resurrection of Jesus.
- The gospel must be embodied within community.

Furthermore, this robust gospel points out that submission to Jesus leads to salvation, a notion that is more expansive than many understand it to be. Salvation is liberation, and that does not simply mean going to heaven when we die. Liberation is for now as well as later. Salvation affects the present while reaching fulfillment in the future.

THE POWER OF GOD FOR SALVATION

Salvation is liberation. The gospel of Jesus Christ is about salvation. The good news of Jesus Christ means freedom from the slavery of sin. Most of my life I was taught that sin's enslavement was evident only in my personal shortcomings—my failure to measure up to a holy standard, because I kept "missing the mark" (the meaning of *hamartia*, one of the Greek words in the New Testament typically translated as "sin"). Preachers in my world constantly pointed to the need for Jesus to free me from my bad habits, my evil thoughts, and my neglect of upright actions—my sins of commission as well as omission. I preached that same idea hundreds of times. It took me a while to add a critical piece to that message of salvation. I came to believe that sin is not just my inability to live up to a standard, such as the Ten Commandments, or my powerlessness to meet the moral expectations of pious Christians. Sin is deeper than those things prohibited by my childhood church, such as tapping my foot to secular music, attending a party where alcohol is served, or playing card games on Sunday. Sin is more profound than using profanity, smoking cigarettes, or seeing an R-rated movie. Sin is uglier, more pervasive, and more dangerous than individual failings. I came to see that sin is an all-encompassing, cosmos-permeating, creation-destroying force animated by Satan. Sin is indeed the force that exploits my human limitations, resulting in my failures (Romans 6:17-23; Galatians 4:3). But sin is even more than that. Sin is the evil that infiltrates the entire world (Ephesians 2:2). Sin energizes oppressive structures, like fascism, racism, and patriarchy. Sin enslaves people. Sin enslaves animals. Sin enslaves the environment. Sin is slavery for all of creation. Consequently, creation needs liberation. Creation needs salvation. Creation needs Jesus.

Jesus saves. Jesus saves me from what I do that is wrong, but Jesus also saves me from the wrong that is done to me. If the gospel we preach does not address the evil that oppresses people, then it is not good news for everyone. As Christian activist Lisa Sharon Harper asserts, "If one's gospel falls mute when facing people who need good news the most—the impoverished, the oppressed, and the broken—then it's no gospel at all."[1] Those whose theological perspectives have been ignored, whose liturgical practices have been mocked or reduced to entertainment for whites to appropriate, or whose voices have been silenced by other Christians need to embrace and propagate the gospel that is more than personal sin management. A more robust gospel brings power to marginalized people, who must not wait for white people to yield their power and privilege. I often hear well-meaning preachers and teachers urging Christian leaders to "empower" others. I no longer use such language. The power of the gospel comes from God, not from other humans—particularly not from those who fear losing control and influence.

Gospel is synonymous with *evangel,* a word derived from the Greek *euangelion,* meaning "good proclamation," or "good news." While *euangelion* was used in antiquity to describe various types of announcements meant to educate or even warn, currently the word is mostly used to describe the story of Jesus as well as to name the four New Testament writings that tell of his life: Matthew, Mark, Luke, and John. What God offers humanity, in the person and work of Jesus Christ, is good news. However, the way that the gospel has been presented and the manner in which Christianity has often been enacted suggest that the gospel is not good news for everyone. Abolitionist Frederick Douglass offered these famous words:

> What I have said respecting and against religion, I mean strictly to apply to the *slaveholding religion* of this land, and with no possible reference to Christianity proper; for, between the Christianity of this land, and the Christianity of Christ, I recognize the widest possible difference—so wide, that to receive the one as good, pure, and holy, is of necessity to reject the other as bad, corrupt, and wicked. To be the friend of the one, is of necessity to be the enemy of the other. I love the pure, peaceable, and impartial Christianity of Christ: I therefore hate the

corrupt, slaveholding, women-whipping, cradle-plundering, partial and hypocritical Christianity of this land.[2]

North American Christianity has been hypocritical, particularly regarding its misuse of power. Unfortunately, what Frederick Douglass observed and articulated so eloquently in 1845 resonates with contemporary forms of Christianity. Of course, the formal institution of slavery has been outlawed, but the attitudes that generated and supported the horrible institution are still present. White nationalist groups have been emboldened in recent years, particularly during the Trump administration. In fact, days before I wrote these words, there was another spate of arsons of historic African American church buildings, this time in Louisiana.[3]

The commingling of nationalism and Christianity created a civil religion that not only upheld slavery and patriarchy, but also contributed to the genocide of Native Americans and the marginalization of others who were not considered white. In recent years, predominately white Protestant denominations, such as the Southern Baptists, have issued apologies for their past support of slavery. Even so, branches within North American Christianity continue to give tacit—but also sometimes outspoken—approval of racist and patriarchal ideologies. It might be understandable if the power problem were present in only a small segment of North American Christianity. Sadly, it is not. Evangelicalism, which represents the largest portion of Protestantism, continually demonstrates evidence of its power problem. The so-called Bible Belt, that part of the country most known for its evangelical religiosity, is also notorious for its racism and sexism. That's not a coincidence. During my decades of ministry, I have often had the occasion to preach about or lead discussions on issues of race and power. Inevitably, someone in the group would conclude that such problems would go away if people would simply become Christians, or "believe the gospel." While I appreciated the hopefulness behind such comments, I had to point out the naivete. The gospel of personal sin management, as practiced in our country, serves to preserve the dominant status of white men. When people confess belief in propositions about the death and resurrection of Jesus, they do not automatically awaken to the reality of societal evils. Furthermore, if people who confess belief in propositions about Jesus remain within mainstream evangelicalism, they are unlikely to acknowledge the realities of racism and other systemic evil.

THE POPULAR NORTH AMERICAN GOSPEL

Millions of people in the USA self-identify as Christian, yet perpetuate the power problem within Christianity. They act as if those who claim to take the Bible seriously—even literally—cannot possibly be party to the oppression of others. Christians may fall into the trap of thinking that only hooded Klansmen are racists, or that those like Archie Bunker (the iconic '70s sitcom character known for his bigotry and sexism) are the problem. Consequently, we have numerous books, articles, television shows, and movies targeting hardcore racists with the hope of changing their views. The problem isn't with the hardcore sinners; it's with those who don't realize that the problem goes much deeper. Recall the rebuke from Dr. Martin Luther King Jr. in his monumental "Letter from Birmingham Jail":

> First, I must confess that over the last few years I have been gravely disappointed with the white moderate. I have almost

reached the regrettable conclusion that the Negro's great stumbling block in the stride toward freedom is not the White Citizens' Counciler or the Ku Klux Klanner, but the white moderate who is more devoted to "order" than to justice; who prefers a negative peace which is the absence of tension to a positive peace which is the presence of justice; who constantly says "I agree with you in the goal you seek, but I can't agree with your methods of direct action"; who paternalistically feels he can set the timetable for another man's freedom; who lives by the myth of time and who constantly advises the Negro to wait until a "more convenient season."[4]

Christianity's power problem is the result of well-intentioned Christians who fail to understand or appreciate systemic evil—the sin that permeates all human structures. Walking the aisle in response to an altar call, attending Bible studies, reciting Bible verses, or avoiding adultery or particular peccadillos does not guarantee a person's grasp of the gospel of Jesus Christ. The issue is not about attempting to identify and then weed out those who appear to be blatant racists; there may be a problem with the entire garden. Therefore, we need to explore the dynamics under the surface that undergird Christianity's power problem. A person's understanding of the gospel of Jesus Christ directly influences that person's view and use of power. If the gospel is thought to be a set of propositions about Jesus, then no matter how much people claim to believe those propositions, there is still a good chance that their behaviors will be influenced by other factors such as politics or the attitudes of family members and peers. If the gospel, however, is more than propositions, and involves a radical change in one's allegiance and commitments, then there is a greater likelihood of reducing the impact of the power problem.

During my years planting a church in Brooklyn, New York, I periodically walked around my neighborhood, sometimes with church folks from our new church as well as with visitors from outside NYC. It was our intention to evangelize anyone we might meet. We hoped to have conversations with strangers, and engage them in the content of the evangelical booklet *The Four Spiritual Laws*. I have a vivid recollection of meeting a man who was sitting at a stone table in a park. It was early on a Saturday morning, and he appeared to be tired, and had likely been sleeping in the park. He was disheveled and unshaven and had a backpack on the ground next to him. He welcomed my presence when I asked if he had some time to talk with me. I talked through the booklet as I had been taught and got to the page with two circles. Both circles had the picture of a chair at the center. On one chair was a symbol to indicate *self*, and the other circle had a cross on the chair to symbolize Christ. The *self* circle had a series of dots that were random and disordered to indicate that human thoughts and interests are chaotic when we are in charge of our own lives. The circle with the cross on the chair showed dots that were organized, radiating in straight lines from the chair. This was to indicate that with Christ "on the throne of our lives," our thoughts and interests would fall into place. Our lives could have meaning with Jesus at the center.

When I got to the picture of those circles, I invited the man to pray for Jesus to be on the throne of his life. Even back then I did not want my presentation to be about a list of propositions; I wanted it to be about a commitment to Jesus. However, I'm not sure my overall presentation was helpful. The man did pray. Yet I recall the feeling of powerlessness I had at that moment. There were friends of mine who would be excited for me that the man prayed the prayer in the booklet. For them, that was the goal of my interaction with that man. But I kept noticing how distressed he appeared. He needed circumstances to change. He didn't seem concerned about having his thoughts and activities fall into an orderly pattern; he needed the basics of life itself. I did not have much to offer him at that moment, and I contented myself with an idea that had been fed to me: the gospel was about the man's heart, not his circumstances. If our church had a program to help him, that would be great, but the most important work had been done.

I have too many memories of interactions such as the one I had in the park that day. What I came to see was what many Christians before me had already seen, but whose voices were denounced in the evangelical settings where I had been trained. I came to see that those whose backs are against the wall don't need to know that Jesus brings order to their disordered lives; they need deliverance from the system that oppresses them.

The gospel is good news because Jesus said he came to set captives free, to give sight to the blind, to heal the broken-hearted, and to usher in the Jubilee (Luke 4:18-19). The apostle Paul says Jesus makes all things new (2 Corinthians 5:17). The gospel should not be reduced to a set of ideas. The gospel isn't just something that we read or recite. The gospel isn't just something that we hear. The gospel must also be seen. The gospel is a way of life that looks like the life of Jesus. And Jesus said that people would know that we are his disciples when they can see the love that we have for each other. While there is a tendency among many evangelicals to reduce the gospel to proclamation (perhaps while recognizing resultant good works), it is not likely that the earliest Christians—including the apostle Paul—would have separated proclamation about Jesus from the actions performed and urged by Jesus (see John 14:15; Galatians 5:6; 1 John 5:2-3). The New Testament teaches that the gospel is a way of life that must be embodied, as it involves being *in Christ* and becoming "participants of the divine nature" (2 Peter 1:4).

THE GOSPEL IS THE STORY OF JESUS

The gospel is a story, not a set of propositions. I used my experience with *The Four Spiritual Laws* as an illustration, but I realize that the booklet was a product of a particular period in the history of North American evangelicalism, and I respect that the late Dr. Bill Bright created the booklet as a tool for evangelism. However, we need to embrace a more robust gospel, one that centers the life of Jesus as well as his death and resurrection. The more we come to appreciate how powerful the gospel is, the less we will have to fear. The dominant culture need not fear that losing their social hegemony means that they will in turn become oppressed. Those who are oppressed and marginalized need not fear the repercussions of speaking up and acting out. A more robust gospel pays attention to the four gospels and other writings in the New Testament, including the words of the apostle Paul.

New Testament scholar Matthew Bates, upon examining several passages from the pen of the apostle Paul (Romans 1:1-5, 16-17; 1 Corinthians 15:1-5; Philippians 2:6-11), asserts that "*the gospel is the power-releasing story of Jesus's life, death for sins, resurrection, and installation as king.*"[5] The story of Jesus' life includes his Jewish identity, something that often gets overlooked in our thinking about Jesus. In order for the state church in Nazi Germany to support Hitler and his murderous "final solution," Christians had to find ways to disconnect

Jesus from Judaism.[6] Yet even in current times, Christians need constant reminders that Jesus was Jewish, a member of the family of God's people, descended from the matriarch Sarah and patriarch Abraham. Jesus is constantly being made in one's own image, and for the dominant culture that means Jesus was blond, blue-eyed, and for all intents and purposes, American. The popular *Head of Christ* painting by Warner Sallman, with its Roman-nosed, long-haired Lord in three-quarter profile, still persists as the prominent picture of Jesus in the USA, having had a long tenure hanging in churches and homes—even those of African Americans. Recent New Testament scholars emphasize that Jesus was Jewish, and that his life on earth must be connected to the larger history of Israel, especially as told in the Old Testament. Years earlier, African American theologian Howard Thurman emphasized the Jewish heritage of Jesus as a point of hope for those on the margins. During a trip to India, Thurman was confronted by a Hindu leader during a meeting. That leader asserted that Thurman was a "traitor to all the darker peoples of the earth" for becoming a Christian when Christianity had endorsed segregation, lynching, and other forms of terrorism.[7] Thurman's apologetic for why African Americans can be Christians starts with identifying Jesus as a Jew. He writes, "It is impossible for Jesus to be understood outside of the sense of community which Israel held with God."[8]

The story of Jesus is the story of God, the Son, taking on human flesh—the incarnation. Jesus chose to take on the flesh of a marginalized people, even "taking the form of a slave" (Philippians 2:7). Jesus was born to unimpressive parents from an unimpressive town (John 1:46). The Lord identified with people under the yoke of Roman oppression. Furthermore, he chose to have personal fellowship—even over meals—with those ostracized by their own people, such as tax collectors and other notorious sinners (Matthew 9:10; Luke 19:7). To illustrate the Lord's humble life on earth, his birth is set in contrast to the reign of Caesar Augustus (Luke 2:1-7). Augustus, the adopted son of Julius Caesar, was called son of god, but the genuine Son of God would be born in a manger, not a palace. The way Jesus chose to enter the world—as a vulnerable child, under arguably unsanitary conditions, to simple parents of a marginalized people, to reach adulthood in a region with an unsavory reputation—is part of the story. It is true that we are called to believe in a Savior who died for humanity, but it is also true that we are called to emulate a Savior who set aside divine privileges for the sake of sinners (Philippians 2:1-8). We must also note the dignity that Jesus gives to people on the margins by choosing to become such a person himself.

THE GOSPEL INCLUDES THE TEACHINGS AND ACTIONS OF JESUS

The first words of the Gospel according to Mark are "The beginning of the good news of Jesus Christ, the Son of God" (Mark 1:1). The expression "good news of Jesus Christ" could be understood in primarily two different ways: (1) good news *about* Jesus, or (2) good news *preached by* Jesus. Jesus is either the content of the good news, the object of the one talking or writing, or the purveyor of the good news. Some scholars suggest both ideas are present. For example, Michael J. Gorman asserts, "We might even say that Jesus not only *proclaimed* the good news to the poor that was promised by Isaiah, but he also *became* that gospel."[9] Jesus is the content of the gospel, and that includes his teaching and actions as well as his death and resurrection.

The book of Acts surely emphasizes the proclamation of the gospel message, but it also stresses how actions regularly accompanied preaching. "Signs and wonders" is the term used to describe the miraculous work done in the name of Jesus that corroborated the verbal witness of the apostles and other evangelists (e.g., Acts 2:43; 5:12; 14:3; 15:12). The apostle Paul wrote to the church at Rome, "For I will not venture to speak of anything except what Christ has accomplished through me to win obedience from the Gentiles, by word and deed, by the power of signs and wonders, by the power of the Spirit of God, so that from Jerusalem and as far around as Illyricum I have fully proclaimed the good news of Christ" (Romans 15:18-19). As biblical scholar Craig Keener observes, Paul seems "to believe that miracles happened virtually everywhere he preached."[10] Apart from Pentecostal and other charismatic communities within Christianity, there is a tendency to downplay the signs and wonders presented in the book of Acts. Even so, the apostle Paul describes his ministry thusly to the church in Rome: "By the power of signs and wonders, by the power of the Spirit of God, so that from Jerusalem and as far around as Illyricum I have fully proclaimed the good news of Christ." Paul says that his proclamation includes signs and wonders by the Spirit of God. In fact, the power of Paul's preaching came not through impressive rhetorical skill, but with demonstration of the Spirit (1 Corinthians 2:1-5).

Our communication of the good news of Jesus must also be connected to a demonstration of God's activity as the Holy Spirit works through God's people. Evangelists in developing countries, as well as in rural and urban areas of the USA, have long known that the proclamation of the good news of Jesus cannot be divorced from Spirit-empowered efforts to alleviate

suffering. These efforts can be contemporary signs and wonders. Healthcare, legal support, food, clean water, clothing,
shelter, and advocacy are the types of efforts needed to bring
dignity to those who suffer, much like Jesus did when curing
leprosy or giving disabled beggars the ability to walk. Signs and
wonders in the name of Jesus are not attempts to earn God's
favor. Rather, they are part and parcel of what constitutes the
good news of Jesus.

THE GOSPEL INCLUDES LIBERATION FROM SIN
THROUGH THE DEATH AND RESURRECTION OF JESUS

There are numerous metaphors to describe the impact of what
Jesus did on the cross. One image that appears in the New
Testament is that of ransom, or redemption. Jesus said these
words: "For the Son of Man came not to be served but to
serve, and to give his life a ransom for many" (Mark 10:45).
These two quotations from New Testament letters are among
several that discuss the redemption, or ransom, of Jesus: "You
know that you were ransomed from the futile ways inherited
from your ancestors, not with perishable things like silver or
gold" (1 Peter 1:18), and "For there is one God; there is also
one mediator between God and humankind, Christ Jesus,
himself human, who gave himself a ransom for all—this was
attested at the right time" (1 Timothy 2:5-6).

The words translated "ransom" and "redemption" are ety-
mologically related. When we hear the word *ransom* we tend
to think of money paid to kidnappers to get someone back.
The word *redemption* might cause us to think in a typically
American commercial way, focusing on the pawnshop, where
people buy back an item that has been held as collateral. But
for people in the first century CE, when they heard the word

ransom or *redeem*, they didn't focus on money per se, but on freedom. First-century people thought of the release of a captive, or the freeing of a slave. Slavery was a very common part of life in the ancient world, and those who first heard the words of the New Testament were familiar with the practices of slavery. Redemption is freedom. Redemption and ransom mean "release" and "rescue."

THE GOSPEL MUST BE EMBODIED WITHIN COMMUNITY

It is impossible to follow Jesus in isolation. The Christian faith is a communal faith. Together we communicate that God is real, that Jesus saves, and that the Holy Spirit transforms. People outside the community of faith will recognize us as followers of Jesus when we demonstrate our mutual love (John 13:35). The good news of Jesus compels believers in Jesus to pursue fellowship with each other. The Lord's chief command is that we love God and love others (e.g., Mark 12:30-31). Obedience to that command requires community. The rest of this book is largely an encouragement to embody the gospel in the face of injustice. In the USA, Christians of color can unite to turn the tables on injustice. Onlookers will be able to see Jesus in how we serve in a variety of contexts, work through differences, peacefully oppose evil, and worship with our entire being.

two

The Power of Diaspora People

Beloved, I urge you as aliens and exiles to abstain from the desires of the flesh that wage war against the soul. Conduct yourselves honorably among the Gentiles, so that, though they malign you as evildoers, they may see your honorable deeds and glorify God when he comes to judge.

—1 PETER 2:11-12

WHEN NEW COMMUNITY, the church we started in our apartment in Brooklyn, New York, finally found a place to use on a daily basis, our young congregation was thrilled. Before that time we had worshiped in an Episcopal church's fellowship hall, which was available to us only on Sunday afternoons and evenings. But that had been an improvement over holding worship services in our apartment. The new worship location was the storefront building on the first floor of our apartment building. The landlord was happy to have my family responsible for paying the rent on two of the three units in his building. Shortly after we signed the lease, before we had a sign on the building, I was locking up one evening and saw a car racing down the street, heading in my direction. Locking up involved bolting the doors, of course, but also pulling down a large grate in front of the building and securing it with a padlock. I moved quickly to secure the grate, not sure of what was going on. The car bounced over the curb and drove right up onto the sidewalk a few feet from me. My heart raced as I turned the corner with my keys out, ready to enter the stairway up to our apartment. Right as I was about to get the key into the door, I sensed a flashlight on me. I was ordered to stop. Several men in ordinary clothes were facing me. I recall one man had a flashlight and the others had their hands on the revolvers on their hips. I still don't recall the men identifying themselves as police, but they angrily asked me what I was doing at the "store." It took me a minute to realize that they were talking about our new church space. I had my hands up, hoping they could see that what was in my hand were keys, and not a weapon. Fortunately, I was able to explain what I was doing, and after what seemed like a lengthy time of visual scrutiny, the policemen said I could go.

Ethnic minorities are often hypervigilant, especially when the police are near. It seems that on too many occasions our presence sends a threatening message to white people and police officers. Consequently, many of us are careful to eliminate as much scrutiny from the dominant culture as possible. We notice the nervous looks when we group ourselves in public spaces, or when the volume of our conversation rises. We teach our young people—especially the boys and young men—to be prepared for what might happen when driving while black. Diaspora people are always struggling to fit in without adopting all the values of the dominant culture. That struggle to fit in reflects what is happening behind the scenes of the Scripture passage cited above.

The first readers of the letter 1 Peter were alienated from the dominant culture. They are described as members of the diaspora (1 Peter 1:1). As followers of Jesus, the Christian community to which Peter writes was out of step with the broader society. They struggled to live the Lord's teachings while being mocked, slandered, and otherwise alienated by their unbelieving neighbors. Howard Thurman describes well the liminal position of diaspora people when he describes Jews under the Roman Empire as well as African Americans in the USA: "In essence, Rome was the enemy; Rome symbolized total frustration; Rome was the great barrier to peace of mind. And Rome was everywhere. No Jewish person of the period could deal with the question of his practical life, his vocation, his place in society, until first he had settled deep within himself this critical issue. This is the position of the disinherited in every age."[1]

Diaspora Christians are the disinherited and possess unique power to demonstrate the way of Christ.

> The solution which Jesus found for himself and for Israel, as they faced the hostility of the Greco-Roman world, becomes the word and the work of redemption for all the cast-down people in every generation and in every age. . . . The basic fact is that Christianity as it was born in the mind of this Jewish teacher and thinker [Jesus] appears as a technique of survival for the oppressed. That it became, through the intervening years, a religion of the powerful and dominant, used sometimes as an instrument of oppression, must not tempt us into believing that it was thus in the mind and life of Jesus.[2]

Thurman knew that the disinherited have the power to reveal what genuine Christian faith is. Diaspora Christians, those who don't quite fit into the dominant culture, are among the best teachers of what it means to follow Jesus.

DIASPORA CHRISTIANS

In the recent past, *Christianity Today*, as well as other evangelical publications, frequently ran ads for Christians to find their "family crest." People could submit their surnames to some company in order to discover their family crest: a coat of arms heralding a particular genealogical clan, usually of Scottish, Irish, or British background. The company that provided such a service understood that there would be a market among white evangelicals to connect to their European roots. My last name is Edwards, which I am sure is an English name, but I will likely never know how I came to have this name. Given slavery's legacy in the New World, which caused the breakup of families, thereby erasing genealogical connections, many African Americans cannot accurately trace our roots to any country in Africa. Genetic tests, such as those offered by Ancestry or 23andMe, yield only general results, covering broad regions of Africa. The identity of black people in the USA is tied to the entire continent of Africa, so we are called African American, in contrast to those who can name a particular country, such as Norwegian American, or Italian American. African Americans are among those people dispersed from the homeland, and our history in the United States is not glamorous. Africans in Europe and the Americas are products of a *diaspora*, a dispersion—often forced—of a people group outside their homeland.

Marginalized believers—what we could call *diaspora Christians*—are generally the best practical guides as to what it means to be followers of Jesus Christ. Contemporary Christian America—as divided, as arrogant, as theologically selective, and (surprisingly) as beloved by God as it is—needs to learn from marginal Christian voices. The rally of white supremacists in Charlottesville, Virginia, in 2017, as well as other similar events, demonstrated the presence of the white nationalism that has always been part of the fabric of America. The Ku Klux Klan and other white supremacist groups are not an aberration; they're an extreme form of what many in the country have believed since its founding. And to make matters worse, Christianity itself has been intertwined with nationalism. As the 2016 presidential election demonstrated, white Christians have long enjoyed social hegemony—even a sense of entitlement. New York minister Jonathan Walton describes aspects of the sense of entitlement that white Christianity reinforces, labeling it part of white American folk religion, or WAFR.[3] One of the tenets of WAFR, according to Walton, is the practice of "covert and overt efforts to uphold a race-, gender- and class-based hierarchy."[4] White American folk religion, or whatever we call it, is the system that establishes and reinforces the sense of entitlement that is pervasive among Christians of European ancestry in the USA.

The people who first received the New Testament letter called 1 Peter were marginalized believers, and these believers serve as examples for us today. As noted, the recipients of 1 Peter are addressed as diaspora people in the first verse of the letter. Marginalized believers—even today—are like Peter's people; they are a diaspora people. Christians within the dominant culture have much to learn from diaspora Christians—those followers of Jesus whose perspective does not come from the top but has been shaped from the side or the bottom of society.

Our Lord Jesus was a voice from the margins, and he shows that such a place can be one of honor and not shame. Because Jesus himself experienced life on the margins, it is fair to say that diaspora Christians are in a unique position to model the way of Jesus.

Discerning the way of Jesus among the most vulnerable seems simple and straightforward, and I think many of us sense that it is right. Yet it goes against the way of our world. We have been conditioned to bypass the lowly, and virtually ignore those who do not have status in the eyes of most people. It will take some retraining for Christians to learn their lessons and take their cues from those who are not part of the dominant culture. Listening to the voices of the oppressed, or simply providing a token place for them to vent their frustrations, is not enough. If we are willing to be retrained, however, with a posture of humility, I am confident that God will breathe a fresh wind of the Spirit into the church. If we are willing to have ears to hear and eyes to see, we will demonstrate to the broader world the countercultural gospel that changes lives and transforms societies.

THE MOST VULNERABLE CAN SHOW US THE WAY OF JESUS

Diaspora is a vulnerable state. In his commentary on the book of Acts, theologian Willie Jennings describes the precarious position of diaspora people:

> Diaspora means scattering and fragmentation, exile and loss. It means being displaced and in search of a place that could be made home. . . . Danger and threat surround diaspora life. . . . The peoples who inhabit diaspora live with animus and violence filling the air they breathe. They live always on the verge of being classified enemy, always in evaluation of their productivity to

the empire, always having an acceptance on loan, ready to be taken away at the first sign of sedition. They live with fear as an ever present partner in their lives, the fear of being turned into a *them, a dangerous other, those people* among *us*.[5]

Jennings captures the vulnerable condition of diaspora people who survive according to the whims of the dominant culture. Peter calls his readers aliens and exiles (1 Peter 2:11). Diaspora people don't confuse faith with nationalism. Aliens, by definition, live outside the mainstream. Peter's readers, as with immigrants throughout time, were socially disconnected from the dominant culture. These Christian believers were alienated from a hostile society. However, despite the unsettled situation of Peter's readers, the letter goes on to affirm their relationship with God:

> But you are a chosen race, a royal priesthood, a holy nation, God's own people, in order that you may proclaim the mighty acts of him who called you out of darkness into his marvelous light.

> Once you were not a people,
>   but now you are God's people;
> once you had not received mercy,
>   but now you have received mercy. (1 Peter 2:9-10)

Those whom Peter describes as God's own people were followers of Jesus who endured harassment, slander, and persecution by the broader society. These marginalized people were the people of God who had received mercy from God. They were nobodies who became somebodies—through the mercy of God! And even though they had been oppressed, these people will bring God glory. That is the way it works with the Lord. He takes those who are weak in the world's eyes to demonstrate his power. He takes what appears foolish to demonstrate his wisdom (cf. 1 Corinthians 1:27-28).

Religion professor Albert J. Raboteau addresses the particular diaspora situation of African Americans in a way that speaks to our ability to model authentic Christian faith.

> African-American Christianity has continuously confronted the nation with troubling questions about American exceptionalism. Perhaps the most troubling was this: "If Christ came as the Suffering Servant, who resembled Him more, the master or the slave?" Suffering-slave Christianity stood as a prophetic condemnation of America's obsession with power, status, and possessions. African-American Christians perceived in American exceptionalism a dangerous tendency to turn the nation into an idol and Christianity into a clan religion. Divine election brings not preeminence, elevation, and glory, but— as black Christians know all too well—humiliation, suffering, and rejection. Chosenness, as reflected in the life of Jesus, led to a cross. The lives of his disciples have been signed with that cross. To be chosen, in this perspective, means joining company not with the powerful and the rich but with those who suffer: the outcast, the poor, and the despised.[6]

We do not always see the way of Jesus in people who have a dominant role in society, but for some reason we keep turning in that direction. We need to turn our heads and look in a different direction. We must see the way of Jesus in those on the margins. "The way of Jesus" refers to the values of the kingdom of God. The way of Jesus is the way of love—of loving God with one's whole being and loving neighbors, even enemies.

The way of Jesus is not a set of propositions; it is a reorientation of one's life. That is what repentance means. The way of Jesus is often best modeled by people on the margins who have discovered that their faith sustains them on the pathway toward full salvation. Look for Jesus among ethnic and racial minorities. He is especially visible there. Look for Jesus among the immigrant population; the Lord is certainly visible there. Look for Jesus among women, who so frequently have been devalued, objectified, and abused, but who remain consistent models of faith under fire. And look even to children to see the way of Jesus. Our Lord himself set children as an example for what the kingdom of God looks like (Mark 10:13-16). Look to diaspora people—those who have been pushed to the margins—in order to discern the way of Jesus.

DIASPORA CHRISTIANS STRENGTHEN THE ENTIRE CHRISTIAN MOVEMENT

The strength of the African American church is well-documented. Under the heat of slavery, Jim Crow segregation, lynching, government-sanctioned discrimination, and various other evils, African American Christians have defied all odds. As a people, we have started churches, denominations, educational institutions, hospitals, banks, businesses, and a host of other resources that not only uplift the African American community but also benefit the rest of society.

The power of diaspora Christians can be seen in the immigrant community as well as among African Americans. Missiologist Soong-Chan Rah describes how immigrant churches help free the church from white cultural captivity. For example, Rah notes how the Korean American church models holistic ministry. "The Korean immigrant church," he writes, "has been the most influential, formative and stable institution in the Korean immigrant community, an institution that has helped to shape Korean American identity."[7] Furthermore, Rah points out how the Korean immigrant ethnic church provides social services for new immigrants as well as for church members generally. Bicultural Americans, according to Rah, should lead in addressing the challenges of multiethnicity.[8] Latinx Christians, for example, have long figured out how to live within majority white culture, moving deftly between worlds. These diaspora Christians are expert teachers of what Christian mission can look like in our time.

Consider that conservative Christians are notoriously anti-immigrant. Communication professor Heather Thompson Day, who works with the Barna Research Group, makes this assertion: "Only 25 percent of white evangelicals felt a responsibility to help people who have been forced to leave their country due to horrifying circumstances. White evangelicals were the least likely of all groups to feel any responsibility for the very same people scripture says in Deuteronomy 10:18-19 that God loves."[9] Immigration is certainly a complex issue, but immigrant Christians may be best able to teach us how to bring the love of God to the matter. Christians who have experienced the challenges and opportunities of moving to a new and strange land can make scriptural admonitions come to light for all of us.

DIASPORA CHRISTIANS DEMONSTRATE RESILIENCE

I recently preached at a multicultural church in Arizona where several Latinx as well as Congolese families attended alongside white people of European descent. At dinner the evening before I preached, one of the pastors informed me that the Congolese members had been refugees. She went on to describe the great faith of the Congolese believers and observed, "We have so much to learn from them." I appreciate the humble posture of that white pastor. She could see that diaspora Christians are teachers because they practice resilience. They model faith under pressure. Diaspora Christians demonstrate tenacious faith in horrible circumstances. Immigrants, as well as we who are the descendants of slaves, know the alienation that stems from unfamiliarity with new settings as well as the xenophobia of the host culture. I am continually amazed at the endurance of African people brought to this country as slaves. I also marvel that many became Christians despite the evils of slavery as well as American Christianity's ambiguous attitude toward slavery. Some Christians fought against slavery while others vigorously defended the right of white people to own other people.

The apostle Peter writes about suffering through difficult trials as part of the faith journey of his readers:

> In all this you greatly rejoice, though now for a little while you may have had to suffer grief in all kinds of trials. These have come so that the proven genuineness of your faith—of greater worth than gold, which perishes even though refined by fire—may result in praise, glory and honor when Jesus Christ is revealed. (1 Peter 1:6-7 NIV)

Diaspora people model the way of Jesus by showing what faithful perseverance looks like and, as Peter says, by rejoicing even through suffering. Diaspora people are often the ones who face alienation and other forms of suffering. Diaspora Christians, oppressed believers, teach us *hypomonē*, the New Testament word for "endurance," or "faithful perseverance."

For example, slaves who were brought from Africa to what would become the United States of America were thrust into an environment heavily influenced by Christianity. Many slaves in America, just like the slaves that Peter addresses (cf. 1 Peter 2:18), are among our best teachers when it comes to faithful perseverance. For example, Negro spirituals were birthed as slaves came to connect their story to the biblical story. The spirituals grew out of the dynamic tension of living with faith in God, who promises deliverance, while simultaneously experiencing the slave master's whip. Although the spirituals were fundamentally work songs that provided some measure of relief from backbreaking labor, they also served to help build a measure of community. The spirituals helped the slaves affirm that they were not defined by their work; their identity was rooted in a spiritual reality that transcended their present circumstances. Plenty of Christians in the dominant culture can learn that their lives need not be defined by their work. African American slaves teach us that there is a spiritual realm that, although typically unseen, is nevertheless real. We are meant to relate to the God of the universe, not the god of work, or the god of sex, or the god of money, or any other idol. Oppressed people teach us that we can—as Peter puts it—abstain from sinful desires that wage war against our souls (2:11). We can live such good lives among unbelievers that, though they accuse us of doing wrong, they may see our good deeds (2:12).

Presently, African Americans, when it comes to income, education, health, and other critical measures, are still worse off than the dominant culture. Some in our society will blame African Americans entirely for the disparities, but rational people know better. We have a long legacy of persevering through suffering. Even though some people get annoyed when we say it, black lives matter to God, even when it doesn't often feel like it on earth. Slaves, and their offspring, do not demonstrate weakness, but rather the power of Jesus.

Slaves—in Peter's day and also in America—didn't live and die in vain. Slaves didn't suffer just to fill the pockets of the powerful. Slaves didn't endure beatings just to pick cotton and tobacco. Slaves didn't get raped and tortured simply to fulfill the dreams of white people. Slaves didn't have their families decimated to make America great. Suffering is not the only legacy of African Americans. God has taken the misery of my forebears, as well as the misery of some of Peter's readers, to shame the powerful. God has taken the evil of human beings and turned it around on them. God has made it so that if we want to see Jesus, we don't look to the powerful; we look to the apparently powerless! If we want to see Jesus, we look to slaves. I wish there never had been slavery, but in light of the history, we see that those who suffered horribly teach us the depth and breadth of resilience.

DIASPORA CHRISTIANS NONVIOLENTLY OPPOSE INJUSTICE

When Howard Thurman pointed out the similarity between Jesus and the disinherited, he acknowledged not only their comparable vulnerable situations, but also their need to practice nonviolent resistance.[10] Violence can never be an ultimate solution to injustice. Violence is not the way of Jesus, even if it appears to be the most advantageous strategy. Peter makes a similar point to his marginalized, oppressed readers. "For to this [suffering] you have been called, because Christ also suffered for you, leaving you an example, so that you should follow in his steps. 'He committed no sin, and no deceit was found in his mouth.' When he was abused, he did not return abuse; when he suffered, he did not threaten; but he entrusted himself to the one who judges justly" (1 Peter 2:21-23).

The civil rights movement in America illustrates Peter's point of how God's people witness to the world by practicing nonviolent resistance. One of the things that made the civil rights movement effective was the way innocent protestors endured abuse and did not retaliate. Dr. Martin Luther King Jr. propagated the notion of nonviolent protest. And although there were some who disagreed with his approach, many look back on history and note that his philosophy, which was at the heart of the movement, drove the legislative changes that inched their way through the government. Rep. John Lewis participated in the protest in Selma, Alabama, on March 7, 1965. He describes the effect it had in catching the attention of the broader society.

> ABC Television cut into its Sunday night movie . . . with a special bulletin. News anchor Frank Reynolds came on-screen to tell viewers of a brutal clash that afternoon between state troopers and black protest marchers in Selma, Alabama. They then showed fifteen minutes of footage of the attack. . . . The American public had already seen so much of this sort of thing, countless images of beatings and dogs and cursing and hoses. But something about that day in Selma touched a nerve deeper than anything that had come before. . . . People just couldn't believe this was happening, not in America. Women and children being attacked by armed men on horseback—it was impossible to believe. But it happened. And the response from across the nation to what would go down in history as Bloody Sunday was immediate.[11]

John Lewis is a hero. There are many civil rights activists, however, whose names the public might never know. We have family members who faced injustice, who took the hits and kept getting up, who witnessed evil but pressed on to do good.

In 2018 I was part of Sankofa journey in the form of a civil rights trip with a group of pastors. "Sankofa" is a word in the Twi language of Ghana that translates to "Go back and get it," and African Americans have applied the word to trips to Africa or to the southern US.

My mother was born in Laurens, South Carolina, in 1928. She was an only child, but her mother was one of twelve siblings. During my lifetime I got to know several of those siblings from Laurens. I often tried to imagine their lives, as they were people born in the late nineteenth and early twentieth centuries who endured the Jim Crow South. The trip down south caused me to reflect soberly on US history, including slavery and the Jim Crow era. During the journey we stopped at the National Memorial for Peace and Justice in Montgomery, Alabama. The memorial recognizes the lives of African Americans who were lynched, victims of domestic terrorism.

The memorial consists mostly of numerous large, rust-colored, metallic, rectangular prisms hanging from the ceiling, each representing a US county and bearing the names of lynching victims. As our group walked through the memorial, these prisms were first at eye level, but as we continued along a downward slope, the prisms rose above us, so we had to look up. This mirrored what a witness to a lynching might experience: seeing the victim face-to-face, but then gradually watching the victim be raised overhead. The group continued outside to where more rectangular metal prisms rested horizontally on the ground; our eyes turned downward, the way one might have to view a dead body.

On one of those hanging prisms I found a list of names from Laurens County, South Carolina, my mother's home. The name at the bottom of the list was "unknown." I wondered about that person's life and the ostensible reason for his or her lynching. Did my family members know that person? Surely they knew about the lynching in their county. Perhaps the terrorizing of African Americans in the South is what caused my mother, my grandmother, and some of her sisters (my great-aunts) to be part of the Great Migration, as they moved from South Carolina to Washington, DC, and also to New York City, taking jobs as domestic servants for white people. Maybe the fear of reviving trauma is what made them reluctant to speak about their lives in the South. Most of the members of my family from Laurens, South Carolina, are deceased, including my mother. I am not able to have conversations with them about the past. One legacy that some of the family members leave, however, is the model of tenacious faith in Jesus while under the broilers of racism and patriarchy. These women in my family—as well as many other unnamed people—are diaspora Christians who show us the way of Jesus.

Those who have been oppressed are the best teachers of the way of Christ. Consequently, I would much rather heed the voice of a slave, or listen to a marginalized immigrant follower of Jesus, than model myself after a Christian leader who boasts of being close to the president of the United States. God's power is evident among diaspora believers. We should honor the legacy of diaspora Christians. They might suffer, but in so doing they show us Jesus.

THREE

The Power to Discern Injustice

Since, therefore, the children share flesh and blood, he himself likewise shared the same things, so that through death he might destroy the one who has the power of death, that is, the devil, and free those who all their lives were held in slavery by the fear of death.

—HEBREWS 2:14-15

SOME OF THE CONVERSATIONS during my years as a student at Cornell University were about the problem of apartheid in South Africa. Many of us young people were eager to see that evil, oppressive, violent, and racist system dismantled, even urging our university to divest from any corporations doing business in South Africa. I was surprised, however, that most of the white Christians I knew were willing to see apartheid continue. The prominent American Christian leader Jerry Falwell Sr. even encouraged Americans to buy gold Krugerrands to bolster the oppressive South African regime.

White Christians I met echoed Falwell's fears that black South Africans—the overwhelming majority of the population—would have the right to govern their country, which had been colonized by Europeans. I vividly recall a white man, involved in a popular Christian group on campus, voicing his concern to me that if black South Africans were to rule their own homeland, they would become Marxists. He cited what he saw as problems associated with Rhodesia becoming Zimbabwe, a transition that had taken place early in my time at Cornell.

White Christians tend toward preserving the status quo, which serves to protect their worldview, their way of life, and their privileged position—even when those positions are acquired through violence and coercion. The Christianity offered by the protectors of the status quo tends to focus on personal ethics, especially issues such as sexual behavior, alcohol consumption, watching movies, and even dancing. The goal appears to be the management of personal sins so as to secure one's place in heaven, or at least not to miss out on any rewards in the afterlife.

The most popular form of Christianity in the USA, and the one with which I am most familiar, is evangelicalism. Evangelicals tend to focus on theological dogma and personal piety, emphasizing sexual restraint along with abstaining from alcohol. Lest that sound like an overstatement, recall that evangelicals gave Prohibition its momentum. In the popular mindset, Christians are mostly known for preaching against particular personal vices such as substance abuse, the use of profanity, and of course, most notably, sexual behavior—including abortion (along with issues that evangelicals tend to associate with sexual behavior: woman's clothing, popular music, and movie ratings). It is rare to hear American evangelicals preach against systemic injustice. In fact, I know white Christians who cringe when they hear the word *justice*. For this form of Christianity, the message to those on the margins of society is to avoid personal sinful behavior and defer to authority. God, it appears, is concerned only about a particular form of morality, and not about oppression.

THOSE WHOSE BACKS ARE AGAINST THE WALL

Howard Thurman offered the following lament:

> I can count on the fingers of one hand the number of times that I have heard a sermon on the meaning of religion, of Christianity, to the man with his back against the wall. It is urgent that my meaning be crystal clear. The masses of men live with their backs constantly against the wall. They are the poor, the disinherited, the dispossessed. What does our religion say to them? The issue is not what it counsels them to do for others whose need may be greater, but what religion offers to meet their own needs. The search for an answer to this question is perhaps the most important religious quest of modern life.[1]

Thurman, notwithstanding his lack of inclusive language, which was consistent with the spirit of his time, offers a critique that is still relevant for much of contemporary white American evangelicalism. That popular form of Christianity typically fails to offer an empowering message to those on the margins. Faithful followers of Jesus have certainly produced much good work over the centuries, building hospitals, schools, and orphanages, attempting to alleviate suffering while demonstrating the love of Christ. Yet despite the many charitable acts performed by Christians through the ages, the message to those on the margins was essentially fatalistic: God had ordained the social order. Thurman was aware that Christians in the USA preached to or about those whose backs are against the wall; the problem was that the message was not empowering, and the messengers were hypocritical.

Christianity is meant to be a liberating faith. Consequently, it should encourage the liberation and empowerment of those whose backs are against the wall. This is not to say that all problems will be solved before Jesus returns. There is certainly a better life to come. Even so, Christianity's message is not "pie in the sky when you die." A failure of North American Christianity is its impotence and even disinterest in giving dignity to those whose backs are against the wall. North American Christianity has a power problem. People on the margins have a unique ability to discern the injustice resulting from American Christianity's power problem.

THE EXAMPLE FROM EXODUS

The archetypical symbol of oppressive power in the Bible is Pharaoh in Exodus 1–15. This is how the nameless pharaoh is introduced in the book of Exodus:

> Now a new king arose over Egypt, who did not know Joseph. He said to his people, "Look, the Israelite people are more numerous and more powerful than we. Come, let us deal shrewdly with them, or they will increase and, in the event of war, join our enemies and fight against us and escape from the land." Therefore they set taskmasters over them to oppress them with forced labor. They built supply cities, Pithom and Rameses, for Pharaoh. But the more they were oppressed, the more they multiplied and spread, so that the Egyptians came to dread the Israelites. The Egyptians became ruthless in imposing tasks on the Israelites, and made their lives bitter with

hard service in mortar and brick and in every kind of field labor. They were ruthless in all the tasks that they imposed on them. (Exodus 1:8-14)

Pharaoh, ostensibly motivated by fear, enslaves the Israelites and eventually advances a strategy of male infanticide (Exodus 1:15-22). Pharaoh typifies leaders throughout history whose fear of others ushered in hideous strategies to degrade, disenfranchise, or even destroy those who were different and presumed to be a threat. Examples of Pharaoh-like oppression are legion, such as the genocide of Jews in Nazi Germany and the terrorism against Africans in the New World. American slavery was possible, at least in part, because Europeans (including the settlers in the New World) perceived Africans to be ignorant, savage, and not fully human. Even Christians held such views, making it possible for missionary efforts and imperialism to work hand in hand.[2]

The book of Exodus introduces us to Moses, the key figure who leads the Israelites to freedom and the development of a monotheistic nation. Moses is God's vessel to display God's opposition to oppressive power. The authors of *A Theological Introduction to the Old Testament* write, "Although Moses plays an important role as revolutionary agent, it becomes increasingly clear that the crucial confrontation is between the liberating power of Yahweh and the oppressive power of Pharaoh. Through a series of plagues, Yahweh's sovereignty is made clear, and the genocidal policies of Pharaoh's tyranny are shown to have cosmic as well as historical consequences (7:1–11:10)."[3] The consequences include God's protection of creation and the vindication of God's character. God liberated Israel. God demonstrated sovereignty over Pharaoh, the nation of Egypt, water, animals, and other natural elements. As God brings plagues upon Egypt, God tells Moses to say to Pharaoh: "But this is why I have let you live: to show you my power, and to make my name resound through all the earth" (Exodus 9:16). Later, before the first Passover, God tells Moses: "And the Egyptians shall know that I am the LORD, when I have gained glory for myself over Pharaoh, his chariots, and his chariot drivers" (Exodus 14:18). God defeats Pharaoh in order to rescue the Israelites, but does so in a way that condemns and shames oppressive power. God is savior, not oppressor. God's nature as savior is evident in Jesus Christ, as the New Testament affirms repeatedly. Indeed, Jesus is shown to be the ultimate Savior, who destroys the works of the devil, just as Yahweh destroyed the works of Pharaoh:

> Since, therefore, the children share flesh and blood, he himself likewise shared the same things, so that through death he might destroy the one who has the power of death, that is, the devil. (Hebrews 2:14)

> The Son of God was revealed for this purpose, to destroy the works of the devil. (1 John 3:8b)

Furthermore, Jesus demonstrates that salvation is because of divine love (e.g., John 3:16). The love that God has for the world is to be evident in his followers, who are invited to love even their enemies (Matthew 5:44).

Oppressive, Pharaoh-like power is in stark opposition to divine liberating power. Those who claim to be followers of Jesus must not participate in any form of oppression, because such behavior contradicts the character of God. In fact, those who confess that Jesus is Lord must be among the most eager to dismantle the forces of evil instead of colluding with them.

Unfortunately, Christianity has a checkered history when it comes to power. Too often those who have professed to be followers of Jesus willingly participated in efforts to degrade, disenfranchise, dehumanize, and even enslave others. Some Christians behaved like Pharaoh, suppressing the voices, movements, and flourishing of other human beings. However, it is not only the Christianity of a bygone era that I'm calling into question.

Currently, as I write this book, Americans and Britons are decrying a loss of civility as Brits are divided over Brexit and Americans are polarized over politics—especially President Donald J. Trump. Civility is lost—a casualty of the culture wars. Amid the tension, there are Christians who act no differently than the broader society, spouting hateful words directed toward immigrants, ethnic minorities, and other Christians. Even those who do not engage in the vitriol pay little attention to the role they play in a stratified society. For example, some who identify as Christian minimize the role that slavery played in the development of the USA, and pay no attention to the lingering impact of the horrible institution, as African Americans continually lag behind whites in areas such as wealth, health, and education. Discriminatory practices in the USA have been legal for much of the country's history, preventing people of color from advancing in society. However, Christians—especially evangelicals—espouse the myth that America is a meritocracy, where individual effort is all that is needed for success. It seems that only ethnic minorities actually believe the myth of the meritocracy, as generally speaking we strive heroically to be taken seriously, while wealth and privilege serve to advance less-qualified white people. Nationalism deafens some Christians to the teachings of Jesus and blinds them to the needs of other human beings. I've witnessed the denials from Christian men as to how they contribute to the oppression of women. White Christians are typically vehement in their refusal to acknowledge white supremacy and the concomitant privilege. As a result, Christianity can be toxic to women and ethnic minorities. Toxic Christianity no longer enforces literal slavery, as was the case with Africans in the New World, but it continues to fuel actions motivated by fear, to incite behaviors that marginalize others, and to harden hearts to the cries of the oppressed. Toxic Christianity exercises the power to ignore prophetic voices who urge repentance and renewal.

DISCERNING MALE, EUROCENTRIC THEOLOGICAL HEGEMONY

In her discussion of feminist biblical interpretation, Barbara E. Reid asserts that "interpreting the Bible is an act of power."[4] The power to interpret the Bible coincides with the power to marginalize others. Brian K. Blount's 2019 address as president of the Society of Biblical Literature contains this observation: "Those who hold interpretive power establish those outside their circle as Other and assign to them the status of Problem and subsequently the problematic task of working their way out of their Otherness by becoming less like themselves and more like those holding such power. In biblical studies, power has long resided in the alleged impartiality and objectivity of historical and literary methods whose positivism inoculates its practitioners from the viral infections of the space from which they conduct their biblical research."[5] Many serious students of the Bible will admit that there is no pure, impartial, or objective interpretation of Scripture. The social location of the reader affects one's understanding of biblical passages.

The authority to interpret the Bible has long been granted—almost exclusively—to men of European descent. The Protestant Reformation challenged the notion that only Roman Catholic priests and scholars could interpret Scripture. Many Reformers attempted to get the Bible into the hands of ordinary people. Consider that Martin Luther translated the entire Bible from Hebrew, Aramaic, and Greek, so that literate Germans could read the Scriptures in their own language. Even so, there continued to be differences among Reformers as to who had the right to interpret the Bible. Some Reformers insisted that only formally educated clergy could arrive at correct interpretations, while others, such as Anabaptists, believed that faithful laypeople who possessed the Holy Spirit could also interpret the Bible. Yet despite the Reformation's efforts to get the Bible into the hands of ordinary believers, the church was no different from other segments of European society that devalued women and dehumanized those of non-European descent. Prominent New Testament scholar Michael J. Gorman asserts that "when Western Protestant Christianity as a whole believed that its perspective on the world and on the faith was the right one (by virtue of its specially 'blessed' location), it was looking out from the perspective of power and privilege."[6] Scholar Shawn Kelley argues that biblical scholarship became racialized as it fed on racialized philosophical ideas.[7] He asserts, "Biblical scholarship became, and in important ways remains, racialized because it appropriates and participates in a series of racialized discourses. This has happened *irrespective of, and sometimes in opposition to, the intention* of the biblical scholar in question. I wish to be clear here. Rather than accusing individual philosophers and scholars (especially twentieth-century scholars) of being racists or anti-Semites, I am arguing that modern biblical scholarship is trapped by the racialized discourse that it employs."[8]

Reid points out that despite their lack of status, "women interpreting the Bible from the lenses of their own experience is nothing new. Throughout the ages women have recounted the biblical stories, teaching them to their children and others, all the while interpreting them afresh for their time and circumstances."[9] Women have been engaging in biblical interpretation for eons, even though they were not formally recognized as having authority to do so. The same has been true for African Americans.[10] Over the years black theology has emerged as a discipline that reflects the unique experiences of African Americans and the Bible. Professor James H. Evans Jr. asserts:

> Black Theology differs from traditional theology in much the same way that African American Christianity differs from the Christianity of Europe and the North Atlantic. Since the first Africans set foot on this soil, people of African descent have had a singularly unique experience in the New World. They brought with them an inherent philosophical heritage, including a distinctive religious sensibility; they encountered the most brutal form of slavery in human history; and they were introduced to North Atlantic Christianity. Because there was no precedent for the experience of people of African descent, they created distinctive ways of conceptualizing and speaking about their ultimate concerns. Black Theology is a continuation of that discursive tradition.[11]

When a student takes a theology or biblical studies course in most seminaries, she will experience the terminology and modes of analysis that center on white, male engagement with the Bible. It is possible, in some seminaries, to take other theology or biblical studies courses, but those will have adjectives in front, such as *feminist, African American, Latinx,* or *post-colonial.*[12] The default, or standard, theology is that inherited from white men of European descent. As I note this reality, I am not attempting to describe white theological views as de facto wrongheaded. The point I am making at the moment is simply the failure of many Christians to acknowledge the source of their theological perspectives and biases. At the very least, Christians in the USA should view their theological perspectives as *always reforming* (to borrow a notion from the Protestant Reformation), and should understand that theology is deficient when it omits the voices of those in the majority world and ignores the interpretations of ethnic minorities and women.

DISCERNING THE PERVASIVENESS OF WHITE SUPREMACY AND PATRIARCHY

I largely focus on racism because I am African American. However, the power problem of Christianity is evident not only in its racism but also in its patriarchy, as well as its favoritism of those who are financially rich, formally well-educated, able-bodied, and physically attractive. Much of the difficulty our culture has with women holding positions of authority, or even receiving salaries equal to those of men, can be traced to Christianity's patriarchal theological perspectives in the USA. Even our legislators—who are predominately white and male— overwhelmingly profess to be Christian.[13]

People at the top of society's pecking order typically view their position as a result of their own ingenuity, creativity, strength, determination, or God-given right, propagating the myth of meritocracy. Those in power find it hard to fathom

that their power and position is the result of a long and enduring history of exploitation and violence. Societies were built for
the success of men, especially white men. For example, when
it comes to racism, Paul Kivel points out that "racism is based
on the concept of whiteness—a powerful fiction enforced by
power and violence. Whiteness is a constantly shifting bound-
ary separating those who are entitled to have certain privileges
from those whose exploitation and vulnerability to violence is
justified by their not being white."[14] The issue isn't just that
white supremacy exists, but that it exists and is accepted within
much of Christianity. Skot Welch and Rick Wilson, in their
book, *Plantation Jesus: Race, Faith, and a New Way Forward*,
discuss the white supremacists' march in Charlottesville,
Virginia, in 2017, noting how "two of the most prominent
self-declared white supremacists in the United States"—participants Richard Spencer and Jason Kessler—"could have just as
easily been deacons collecting offering on Sunday morning."[15]
Most of us are familiar with America's Bible Belt, recognizing
that the geographical area whose residents are known for their
Christian religiosity is also one of the most overtly racist and
sexist parts of the country. That paradoxical reality gets at the
way Christian faith operates among many: nationalism and
Christianity are intertwined, and faith in Jesus means acknowledging certain Bible verses but not a reorientation of one's
entire life.

With regard to patriarchy, unhealthy uses of male power
are often reinforced through violence. Many sociologists "have
studied and proven the connection between the masculine ideals of power and control, and widespread physical and sexual
violence against women and girls. Sociologists who study these
troubling phenomena point out that these are not crimes of

passion, but of power. They are meant to elicit submission and subservience from those targeted, even in what some would consider to be their less serious forms, like street harassment and verbal abuse."[16] White power and male power are not gifts from God; they are corrupt social dynamics.

DISCERNING ARROGANT AND DIVISIVE LEADERSHIP

We deplore Pharaoh's dictatorship, along with that of so many despots like him throughout history, but sadly, there are churches that operate with forms of leadership that approach dictatorships. Sometimes that style of leadership leads to abuse. In February 2019 the Southern Baptist Convention, the largest Protestant denomination in the USA, was pressed to acknowledge its history of covering up or excusing sexual abuse. The sad but sweeping #MeToo movement prompted the #ChurchToo movement, in which some who endured sexual harassment and abuse communicated their stories.

Sexual abuse, however, is not the only type of abusive leadership found in churches. Church attendees have been traumatized by megalomaniacs and their sycophants who take advantage of people financially or in other ways that quash personal expression and growth. In such settings, women and children are often those with their backs against the wall. They are vulnerable and ignored. Noncollaborative leaders are prideful, incompetent, or both, never learning the advantage of teamwork. Some of these leaders develop large followings because of their personal charisma, and also because dictatorships can be efficient. In these settings, however, talented people may be bypassed, especially if they are introverts who are not adept at self-promotion. Others who are often disregarded include those without great financial resources, those without much formal education, ethnic minorities who refuse to suppress their ethnic identity, those who don't conform to popular standards of beauty, and those with physical limitations.

Furthermore, the dominant culture has contributed to antagonisms between different racial and ethnic groups. Journalist Kat Chow tackles the way that Asian Americans and African Americans have often been pitted against each other, noting, "Since the end of World War II, many white people have used Asian-Americans and their perceived collective success as a racial wedge. The effect? Minimizing the role racism plays in the persistent struggles of other racial/ethnic minority groups—especially black Americans."[17] There are white Christians who participate in such polarizing tactics with members of the same ethnic or racial group as well as with those of different groups.

The power to divide and weaken the bonds between ethnic groups extends into the arena of Christian ministry. White Christians—particularly those who express a desire for diversity—tend to invite certain African Americans to preach or sing. Oftentimes the black presence comes off as entertainment, with whites giggling or oohing and aahing at what is treated as an exotic form of worship. In the evangelical world there have been a relative handful of African American preachers and singers who appealed to white audiences, getting the lion's share of invitations into such spaces. It is possible, however, that if the African American guest denounces white supremacy, she or he might be dismissed as "angry" and thereby unworthy of attention. If the church does not face its participation in societal injustice, having preachers of color address white congregations is not necessarily an indication of racial progress.

I have only touched on broad categories of injustice that affect Christians in the USA. Marginalized people have power to discern injustice as we experience it up close and personally. Because the church, as the body of Christ, needs the participation of all its members (1 Corinthians 12:12), Christians who have been on the margins are exercising God-given power in a multitude of ways and are not waiting for the approval of the dominant culture.

FOUR

The Power of Prophecy

*For whenever I speak, I must cry out, I must shout,
"Violence and destruction!" For the word of the LORD has
become for me a reproach and derision all day long. If I
say, "I will not mention him, or speak any more in his
name," then within me there is something like a burning
fire shut up in my bones; I am weary with holding it in,
and I cannot.*

—JEREMIAH 20:8-9

GOD CHOOSES TO SPEAK through human beings to
bring clarity to current events, to warn of impending
disaster, but also to pronounce future blessings. We call such
spokespeople *prophets*. Prophets are not simply soothsayers or
fortune-tellers. Their predictions issue forth as fruit developed
through a relationship with God, often nurtured over time.
Prophets learn how to discern God's voice. They become familiar with God's written Word as well as the way God has worked
throughout history. Growing familiarity with God includes
passion for God's justice. Prophets speak for God, but are not

merely mouthpieces. They are not just lone voices crying in the wilderness, even if the nature of their ministry appears to make them loners—to themselves as well as to others. Prophets are people whose relationship with God and sensitivity to their contexts compel them to speak God's word to anyone who has ears to hear.

The word *jeremiad* is in our vocabulary because of the biblical prophet Jeremiah, who was given the moniker the Weeping Prophet. Jeremiah reluctantly accepted the call from God to deliver straightforward messages about God's plan to tear down and rebuild God's people (Jeremiah 1:1-10). After a series of discouraging events, Jeremiah lamented that God had called him to deliver harsh messages. Jeremiah said, "I have become a laughingstock all day long; everyone mocks me. For whenever I speak, I must cry out, I must shout, 'Violence and destruction!'" (Jeremiah 20:7b-8a). Jeremiah realized, however, that he could not hold back. Something burned inside him. He could not help but speak the word of the Lord. Such is the call upon genuine prophets. They do not prophesy for personal gain of any kind—money, fame, power, or prestige. They cannot but speak the things that they have seen and heard (see Acts 4:20).

Biblical scholar Ellen Davis observes that prophets in the Bible engaged in a variety of activities, ranging from public speaking and teaching to artistic work and community service.[1] Davis concludes, "People whom the Bible designates as prophet or as possessing the gift of prophecy engaged in all these forms of work. In word and deed, they interpreted the faith for their time, and equally, they interpreted the times for the faithful."[2] In the Hebrew Bible, prophets arose to draw God's people into a thriving relationship with God, recognizing God's sovereignty over the world. God is king, and God's people needed to realize that. Although God had delivered Israel from slavery, preserved them in their journey through the wilderness, and brought them into the Promised Land, the people still rejected God as king (1 Samuel 8:7). Not many generations after the exodus, Israel begged the prophet Samuel for a human king so that they could be like other nations (1 Samuel 8:5). God allowed Israel to become a monarchy. On the whole, however, Israel's monarchy was disastrous.

In his classic book *The Prophetic Imagination*, Old Testament scholar Walter Brueggemann contrasts Israel's society under the leadership of Moses with that of the monarchy, typified in Solomon's reign. Brueggemann argues that "Moses was mainly concerned with the formation of a countercommunity with a counterconsciousness."[3] Solomon, however, developed the monarchy as "a self-serving achievement with its sole purpose the self-securing of the king and dynasty."[4] The self-serving nature of the monarchy was primarily characterized by affluence, oppressive social policies, and "static religion," with that latter term defined as when "the sovereignty of God is fully subordinated to the purpose of the king."[5] What Brueggemann identifies as the dysfunctions of Solomon's reign are typical of all societies at one time or another. The USA is a prime example of a society in which a relatively small number of people possess the vast majority of the country's wealth. Some of the most notable family dynasties exist on wealth accumulated through the oppression of others. Oppressive social policies have long been part of the USA's history, including genocidal actions against Native Americans, enslavement of Africans, the internment of Japanese American citizens, and separating Latinx families along the southern border. The USA has used religion, particularly Christianity, in much the way Brueggemann describes the Solomonic empire. Through the practice of civil religion, the church has often served the purposes of the state. However, the old adage used to challenge preachers generally is certainly true of prophets specifically: they "comfort the afflicted and afflict the comfortable."

PROPHETS FOR ALL TIMES

The prophets of the Bible have a unique place in God's work in the world. However, the gift of prophecy continues in God's church (see Ephesians 4:11). Even as prophecy continues to serve God's church, there is a diversity of opinion about what prophecy entails. The topic of prophecy is too large to treat in this book, but a few observations are in order regarding different ways that prophecy may be viewed today. Generally speaking, churches tend to view prophecy in three basic ways: (1) foretelling the future, or possessing specific insight into a person or situation; (2) preaching sermons; and (3) addressing current—especially political—events.

In some church circles, like the charismatic ones in which I grew up, prophecy describes the ability to know something about a situation without much, or any, prior information, and then to address that situation with a word from God (this phenomenon is sometimes called having "a word of knowledge"—a reference to the King James Version translation of 1 Corinthians 12:8). Such prophecy is characteristic of television preachers who turn to the camera and describe particular illnesses or specific tragedies and then forthrightly assert the manner in which God will cure or deliver. By mentioning television preachers, I merely intend to offer a common illustration, not to cast doubt on the legitimacy of this form of prophecy. While there are certainly charlatans, there are also those who have provided strangers with godly insight on private matters.

For example, during my college years as a chemical engineering student, I had the opportunity to work several months for the Union Carbide Corporation in Charleston, West Virginia. I attended a weekly Bible study at the home of someone who was not connected to the church where I worshiped on Sundays. After several weeks at the Bible study, the pastor who did the teaching took me aside and forthrightly asserted, "God wants you to give up engineering and go into ministry." I asked this pastor several questions for clarification, but left with no intention of giving up my plans to be an engineer. The twists and turns of life are indeed complex, and you probably figured out that I did indeed follow a call from God into church ministry. I did that after I received a bachelor of science in chemical engineering and worked a few years as a math and science teacher. I hasten to point out that this pastor did not have a charismatic theological perspective. He may not have viewed his words to me as prophecy, but I do. That pastor gave me a specific word from God.

In biblically conservative circles, *prophecy* is virtually synonymous with *preaching*. The emphasis is on *forthtelling* rather than *foretelling*. Certainly, most of the words of biblical prophets involved forthtelling—bringing the word of God to bear on current events. However, there is also a clear element of prophetic foretelling that gets overlooked or minimized in some Christian contexts today. Because prophecy can be subjective, the conservative tendency is to dismiss all of it. Some biblically conservative Christians cite the part of 1 Corinthians 13:8 that declares, "But as for prophecies, they will come to an end," and claim that we've reached the time that prophecies have ended. I share the concern of biblical conservatives that prophecy might disregard all rationality and potentially reflect merely the mood or charisma of the so-called prophet. Oftentimes we are pressed to believe anything—even the ludicrous—as long as it is delivered passionately by an impressive or persistent communicator. I don't, however, want to abandon the idea that God speaks through human beings to condemn particular injustices, to revive godliness among God's people, or to provide specific direction in times of confusion. Prophecy is not magical, but it is mystical. This is to say that God is at work in prophets not to entertain or even amaze, but to do what only the Spirit of God can do, which is not always easy to describe or explain.

The prophets of the Bible—including Jesus—called on God's people to repent, or turn away from sin (e.g., Isaiah 31:6; Jeremiah 3:12; Ezekiel 14:6; Hosea 7:10; Malachi 3:7; Matthew 3:2; 4:17). Contemporary prophets do the same. Biblical prophets also addressed people outside their faith community. For example, Jonah was sent to Nineveh (Jonah 1:1-2). Obadiah addressed Edom (Obadiah 1). Isaiah (in chapters 13–27) addresses injustices of other nations (e.g., Babylon, Assyria, Philistia, and Egypt). Ezekiel (in chapter 25) does similarly, giving oracles against Ammon, Moab, Edom, and Philistia). Prophets do not always confine their messages to their own communities. However, they consistently call for the recognition that wrong has been done, and demand repentance. They plead for God's justice. Prophets also make clear that when God's words of admonition and warning are mocked or otherwise ignored, calamity will surely follow.

A VIEW FROM THE BOTTOM

There are Christians of various perspectives who seem willing to use the word *prophecy* to refer to addressing political realities, popularly described as "speaking truth to power." As noble and just as it might sound to speak truth to power, it isn't always clear what the truth is or who possesses the power. Ellen Davis observes, "Certainly all those who get a salary (including pastors and religious educators), all who pay tax on anything and submit forms and reports to governmental, denominational, or educational bodies—we all participate in large social systems that further complicate and likely compromise our own relationship to power."[6] This is not to say that prophets do not exist, or that preachers must refrain from speaking to and about governing bodies (ecclesial, secular, or otherwise). We must be careful, however, to consider the source of prophecy. Not all who claim to speak for God are actually doing so. They may not be free from their own vested interests.

Once again, consider Jeremiah. He prophesied that the people of God would be taken captive by Babylon, and that the captivity would be for a long time (Jeremiah 28–29). His words clashed with Hananiah, who prophesied that the Babylonian king, Nebuchadnezzar, would fall in a mere two years. Hananiah's words were more positive than Jeremiah's, but Hananiah proved to be a false prophet and died a few months after his pronouncement, presumably as a result of God's punishment (Jeremiah 28:12-17). Prophets are fallible human beings, but they arise with keen insight into personal, societal, and even global matters. They must, however, seek to honor God rather than please people.

Prophets represent the lowly parts of society—the margins. The prophets view life not from the upper echelons of society, but from the bottom. In the Bible, we are typically given general information about the prophets, such as their name, father's name, hometown, and nature of their message (e.g., Jeremiah 1:1-10). We may often be treated to details about their enactments of prophecy. One example is Ezekiel, who performed astonishing acts to dramatize God's message, such as sleeping on his left side for 390 days, and on his right for 40 days (Ezekiel 4:4-6), or burning one-third of the hair shaved from his head and face (Ezekiel 5:1-2). Yet the biblical focus is not on the prophet per se, but on God's message, which is directed toward the decision-makers. Monarchs and priests are often the ones the prophets address. Consider Amos, who delivered words so powerful that many still recite them: "Let justice roll down like waters, and righteousness like an ever-flowing stream" (Amos 5:24). Amos was a lowly shepherd and fig farmer when God called him (1:1; 7:14-15), but he managed to provoke the ire of priest and king (7:10).

As in Old Testament times, prophets today view life from the bottom rung of society. Prophets see what the elite often miss. I already noted in the previous chapter that oppressed people have an uncanny ability to discern injustice. Their vantage point allows them to see the impact of policies and perspectives that those in the dominant culture do not see. Philosopher Charles Mills elaborates on how marginalized people have a better understanding of injustice than those in power. Mills points out that "the term 'standpoint theory' is now routinely used to signify the notion that in understanding the workings of a system of oppression, a perspective from the bottom up is more likely to be accurate than one from the top down."[7]

Prophets emerge from, or at least represent, marginalized people. Our society has witnessed prophets who helped shape the course of the country. I refer specifically to those whose faith in Jesus Christ energized their prophetic words. One example is Frederick Douglass. We know him as a former slave turned abolitionist statesman whose writing, speaking, and overall activism influenced the direction of our country. The title of David Blight's biography of Douglass casts the activist as a prophet: *Frederick Douglass: Prophet of Freedom.*[8] Blight emphasizes how much Douglass drew a parallel between his ministry and that of the biblical prophet Jeremiah.

The work of Ida B. Wells overlapped with that of Douglass, and Wells went on to put her own imprint on US history, particularly pointing out the horrors and injustice of lynching. Indeed, there are many prophets throughout history whose names we may never know, who gave voice to those on the bottom of society. Sometimes those prophets did not have a national platform or influence like that of Wells, Douglass, and Martin Luther King Jr. There are prophets whose ministry is to their family, their church, or their neighborhood, or within some other arena. Such prophetic ministry should not be minimized. We become better humans and more faithful followers of Jesus Christ when we heed the prophets that God graciously sends our way. Even though their words might sting those with prestige and power, they can also be a balm for the suffering.

In 2 Samuel 12:1-14, God sends the prophet Nathan to confront King David. Before this incident, we read of how the king lusted after Bathsheba, the wife of Uriah the Hittite, one of the king's soldiers. King David used his power and sexually exploited Bathsheba. Because of the power differential, many scholars are finally calling this episode *rape* rather than *adultery*. Bathsheba became pregnant, and King David plotted to have Uriah killed. The entire incident provides the most famous counterbalance to the story of young David fearlessly facing the Philistine giant, Goliath. David's boldness as a young man is contrasted with his foolhardiness as an older man. Nathan the prophet tells the king a simple story of how a rich man took advantage of a poor man. The rich man, rather than serve one of his own animals to a guest, took the beloved pet, a ewe lamb, from the poor man's family. David is incensed and demands justice, asserting that the rich man deserves death and should make restitution (2 Samuel 12:5-6). The prophet responds, "You are the man!" (v. 7). There are Nathans all around us, representing the plight of those who are marginalized and taken advantage of. The question remains as to how the prophets and their messages will be received.

PROPHETS HAVE A HARD-KNOCK LIFE

I once heard a story on the radio in which a young dad told of trying to explain Christmas and Easter to his little daughter. He explained to her the life of Jesus, how the Lord went around teaching about God, about love, and working miracles for people. When the little girl asked about the cross, the father said that Jesus had some enemies who did not like what he was doing and had him killed. The father recounted that, sometime later, the Martin Luther King Jr. holiday approached. The little girl asked about Dr. King, and the father explained that he was a good man who tried to get people to love each other and to treat everyone fairly. After pausing to consider all this, the little girl then asked, "Did they kill him, too?"

Prophets have a way of riling the forces of evil. Since prophets communicate God's justice to those who are exploiting others, it comes as no surprise that powerful people will try to silence prophets. Not all who receive prophecy respond as King David did. He turned back to God and made attempts to reorder his life. Sadly, it seems that too often what accompanies the prophets' call to speak truth to power is inevitable backlash from the recipients of the prophecy.

The writer of the New Testament book of Hebrews points out this reality. Hebrews 11, popularly called the Hall of Faith, recounts the names and exploits of many people from the Old Testament who lived *by faith*. However, at the end of verse 32, the author mentions a category, *prophets*, without specific names: "And what more should I say? For time would fail me to tell of Gideon, Barak, Samson, Jephthah, of David and Samuel and the prophets." What follows, in verses 33-38, is a list of high points as well as horrors:

> who through faith conquered kingdoms, administered justice, obtained promises, shut the mouths of lions, quenched raging fire, escaped the edge of the sword, won strength out of weakness, became mighty in war, put foreign armies to flight. Women received their dead by resurrection. Others were tortured, refusing to accept release, in order to obtain a better resurrection. Others suffered mocking and flogging, and even chains and imprisonment. They were stoned to death, they were sawn in two, they were killed by the sword; they went about in skins of sheep and goats, destitute, persecuted, tormented—of whom the world was not worthy. They wandered in deserts and mountains, and in caves and holes in the ground.

Prophets get disrespected at least, and killed at worst.

The book of Hebrews recounts some of the biblical data, but there is a long history of prophets who died for challenging powerful people with the word of God. Indeed, I've already alluded to the assassination of Rev. Dr. Martin Luther King Jr. Dr. King's nonviolent, anti-segregation activism was shaped by his Christian faith, even though many Christians were uncomfortable with him and his message. That discomfort was behind Dr. King's famous "Letter from Birmingham Jail," in which he addressed clergy who were suspicious of his activism and did not want him demonstrating in Birmingham, Alabama. Evangelicalism in the United States currently celebrates Dr. King, but cautiously and selectively, lifting certain quotes from Dr. King's public speeches while ignoring his overall ministry and message. Evangelicals generally denounce Christians who advocate for social justice. Indeed, the cultural hegemony of the USA's evangelicals has allowed them to vilify whatever does not fit their particular social and cultural views. Sometimes prophets are dishonored, even in their hometowns (see Mark 6:4). Dr. King was killed, but he was not silenced. The words of prophets remain alive in order to inspire subsequent generations.

Óscar Arnulfo Romero y Galdámez spoke out boldly against injustice and corruption in El Salvador during the 1970s. He had been appointed archbishop of San Salvador and used the pulpit to denounce violence and the exploitation of the poor. Romero was assassinated while celebrating mass on March 24, 1980. He has since been beatified under Pope Francis, and is known as San Romero. He was a prophet in El Salvador and died as a martyr. There are many within Roman Catholicism, as well as those outside that faith tradition, who are motivated by his life and ministry. Not everyone treated unjustly or who has been assassinated is a prophet. But prophets are not welcome among the powerful and privileged. That group is most threatened by prophets.

In our age of social media, there might be a temptation to confuse fussing with prophecy. It is relatively easy—and safe— to sit at a keyboard and complain. Among my social media contacts are people who are quick to point fingers, cry foul, and denounce the actions and attitudes of others. There are those on social media who judge the actions and even the motives of others without all the facts. Self-righteousness on social media appears to be our prerogative as citizens of the USA, as we try to discern how freedom of speech applies to the Internet. But Christian prophets are more than complainers. Prophets do point out injustice, but they also point out the way to God. Prophets do not fit easily into political categories. When considering who might be a prophet in our time, we should take into account the way that person lives, pay close attention to what that person is saying, and also observe how that person is treated by the dominant culture. We need to pray that God protects prophets, and also that their prophetic words do not fail or lose their force.

PROPHECY MUST NOT BE DESPISED

In the gospel of Luke, as Jesus heads toward Jerusalem for what will be his last days on earth, the Lord offers a lament over the city that includes these words:

> Jerusalem, Jerusalem, the city that kills the prophets and stones those who are sent to it! How often have I desired to gather your children together as a hen gathers her brood under her wings, and you were not willing! (Luke 13:34)

Jesus points out that prophets were part of a divine invitation for God's people to experience divine nurturing. The implication is that heeding the message of the prophets would result in godly care and comfort. However, the city's reputation became that of prophet-killer. Jesus' lament looks to the past but also foreshadows the future, as the Lord himself will be executed just outside Jerusalem when forces within the city conspire to eliminate him.

Evilene, the antagonist to Dorothy in the musical *The Wiz*, has a showstopping number in which she sings, "Don't nobody bring me no bad news!" Of course, no one wants to hear bad news, but guilty people are especially wary of it. Those in the wrong have a tendency to kill the messengers who bring hard news (Matthew 21:33-44). Divine messengers, however, despite bearing harsh messages, are agents of God's grace. Even though prophets are to be welcomed and not vilified or harmed in any way, we continually observe the metaphorical (and occasional literal) shooting of the messengers. For example, when someone points out injustice, such as racism, the one pointing it out is accused of being divisive, of "playing the race card," or of otherwise upsetting the order that appeared to be present. There are too many stories of women who blew the whistle on patriarchy or made charges of sexual impropriety only to have every facet of their lives come under intense scrutiny. People of color have often exposed racism within an organization only to have their own reputations called into question. Sometimes these women and people of color are prophets because their presence and words point out injustice. Their words indicate the opportunities to make some part of the world operate more justly, if we would only listen.

At the end of the Sermon on the Mount, Jesus commends those who not only hear his words, but do them (Matthew 7:24). James, the brother of Jesus, writes that we must avoid self-deception by being doers of God's word and not merely listeners (James 1:22). Furthermore, the apostle Paul admonishes the church in Thessalonica not to despise the words of prophets (1 Thessalonians 5:20). Many of us on the margins play a prophetic role for each other as well as for those in the dominant culture. As we discern toxic forms of Christianity and point out injustice of various types, we communicate that the way of Jesus is the best way. God wants to fix broken people and broken systems. However, we must not be frightened or discouraged when people fail to heed our warnings. Prophets have always been rebuffed. Yet we cannot give up. We must be assured that God speaks through prophets before calamity ensues. If the listeners reject our words, they have rejected God.

FIVE

The Power of Anger

*Be angry but do not sin; do not let the sun go down on
your anger, and do not make room for the devil.*

—EPHESIANS 4:26-27

IF **YOUR CHRISTIAN DEVELOPMENT** was anything like
mine, then you may have been taught to downplay,
disregard, or even demonize your emotions. I had learned
to perceive my episodes of discouragement, doubt, fear, and
anger—to name a few normal human feelings—as evidence of
my failure to have faith in God. Happiness was the primary
evidence of a healthy spiritual life, and that happiness had to be
perpetually maintained throughout all sorts of circumstances.
This happiness had to manifest itself in the ways most members
of the church expected: smiling faces, frequent quotations of
biblical passages, singing uplifting songs, and voicing positive
confessions (i.e., not saying anything that could be interpreted
as negative). Of course, it's not beneficial when negative emotions dominate anyone's way of life. We constantly strive to be
hopeful. After all, we live by faith, not by how things appear

(2 Corinthians 5:7). However, the Scriptures, along with human experience, validate the reality of emotions, including anger. Emotionally healthy people are able to name their positive and negative feelings. Such people also know that they need not be held hostage by their feelings. Humans are able to channel their feelings into positive actions.

What I've just described regarding individual emotions may be extended to groups. This is to say that groups of people may have a collective sense of indignation or anger. In fact, Ephesians 4:26-27, cited above, gives four commands in grammatically plural forms, which is to say that the entire community is being addressed (notice the "one another" language of the preceding verse, 4:25). The commands are: (1) be angry, (2) do not sin, (3) do not let the sun set on what provoked your anger (i.e., deal with the source of your anger straightaway), and (4) do not make room for the devil. Verse 26 invites anger, a natural human reaction to an offense. When we are confronted with evil, anger is among a range of appropriate reactions. We ought not be surprised that when we experience injustice, or merely learn about what others may be facing, our adrenaline pumps harder and our tempers flare. We must make room for those visceral responses, not suppress them. However, we must not allow our feelings to lure us into sinful behavior. The lust for revenge is strong. Our anger does not give us license to commit violent acts, or to find ways to dehumanize others. "Do not repay anyone evil for evil" (Romans 12:17). The way of Jesus is not the way of retaliation, even in the face of injustice, as I noted in chapter 3 (see 1 Peter 2:18-25). Retaliation can range from snarky, pejorative comments on social media all the way to inflicting physical pain onto guilty parties. Yet those who follow Jesus know that evildoers are not actually our enemies, even if they are the ostensible reason for our anger. The real enemies are the forces of wickedness animated by Satan. "For our struggle is not against enemies of blood and flesh, but against the rulers, against the authorities, against the cosmic powers of this present darkness, against the spiritual forces of evil in the heavenly places" (Ephesians 6:12).

However, knowing that our actual enemies are evil spiritual forces does not excuse us from action. Of course, prayer is the main action in which all followers of Jesus engage (I will address that more in chapter 9). In addition to prayer, angry believers must address the cause of their anger. Verse 26 of Ephesians 4 urges action toward the source of the anger, not the anger itself. *Parogismos*, which appears near the end of verse 26, is not the typical word used for *anger* in the New Testament (the typical word is *orgē*). In fact, *parogismos* appears only here in the entire New Testament, but is used in the Septuagint (the Greek Old Testament). *Parogismos* typically refers to an action that provokes anger (e.g., 2 Kings 23:26; Nehemiah 9:18; and the apocryphal Psalms of Solomon 8:9). Addressing the source of anger may take the form of rebuke, in words and deeds, much in the way that Jesus, as well as the Hebrew prophets, firmly denounced hypocrisy and other sins.

According to Ephesians 4:27, the last part of the above quotation, nonaction gives the devil a foothold among believers. Anger without an appropriate outlet creates opportunities for the devil to thwart the unity of any Christian movement. That is evident in marriage. If unresolved anger between two people can destroy an entire family, how much more damage is possible with larger groups of people?

ANGER AND WHITE FRAGILITY

In the same way that patriarchy has the ability to shrug off the concerns of women, white supremacy permits white people to dismiss the concerns of black people and other ethnic minorities. White people—especially evangelicals—have the luxury of turning a deaf ear to anyone they perceive as angry. In fact, "the angry black person" has become a trope, signifying an irrational, militant complainer. It's the epitome of white privilege to disregard the concerns of an entire race of people. My voice has been muted or ignored on several occasions because white people viewed me as angry. Yet I am in good company. Dr. Martin Luther King Jr. was certainly angry over injustice. Dr. King has become acceptable to mainstream Christianity, even though many whites vilified him during his lifetime. On social media, millions of people post pictures and famous quotes from Dr. King, paying little attention to how during King's lifetime, Christians mocked him, dismissed him as angry, and branded him as too radical. Another great icon of the civil rights movement, Malcolm X, gets a bit more respect these days, but is still generally dismissed by whites because he openly expressed his anger over injustice.

In a 1961 radio broadcast, the author James Baldwin said, "To be a Negro in this country and to be relatively conscious, is to be in a rage almost all the time. So that the first problem is how to control that rage so that it won't destroy you." Angry people cannot refrain from speaking the truth about injustice even if the truth hurts some people's feelings. Victims of injustice have the right to be angry, and anger gives birth to activism. There are many avenues that activism may take, ranging from prayer to charitable acts to nonviolent protests to political lobbying. Anger does not necessitate destruction.

Of course, there are those in the dominant culture who are angry that women, ethnic minorities, and sympathetic white people are raising their voices to rebuke the status quo. Wearers of "Make America Great Again" caps might be angry, as they pine for bygone days when white people's actions and attitudes were not questioned in public. Anger could be an appropriate reaction for people who recognize that their way of life is being challenged. However, history indicates that there are disproportionate results of the outworking of anger. Any person could yield to sin, allowing anger to cause destruction and violence. Yet the scale of such destruction is uneven. Because of white people's position of power in society, their anger goes beyond causing mayhem on a local level. White anger impacts policies and systems. For example, lynching was the result of white anger after the Civil War—systematic terror was inflicted on people of color. White anger restricted voting rights for people of color. White anger opposed school desegregation. White anger placed obstacles to home ownership for black people and other people of color. White anger undergirded the violence against peaceful protestors during the civil rights era.

When I moved to Capitol Hill in the mid-1990s to serve a church there, some of the white members of the church pointed toward a few nearby streets, describing them as "sketchy." It turned out these white people were afraid of areas that were predominately African American. These neighborhoods still had not fully recovered from the blight of the late 1960s and 1970s that impacted many urban areas in the aftermath of the assassination of Dr. King. I never heard those fearful people articulate knowledge of the racist policies that gave rise to segregated and blighted neighborhoods. It exacerbates our anger when white people equate their fear of certain neighborhoods to the fear that people of color have toward government-sanctioned injustice. Like James Baldwin, many of us are still angry. We do not have to swallow our anger in order to protect the feelings of white people.

ANGRY JESUS

Some evangelicals allow themselves to dismiss people of color who are angry about injustice, yet the Lord Jesus Christ himself got angry—and his anger was directed toward religious people as well as his own disciples. While the wrath of God is a common theme in the Bible (e.g., Exodus 4:14; Numbers 11:1; Joshua 7:1, and dozens of other instances), the wrath of Jesus is another matter. We know Jesus as love incarnate, and might find it difficult to imagine him being angry. Some might think that Jesus was not angry on earth, but reserves his anger for final judgment. Yet others will acknowledge the Lord's anger—or something close to anger—when he cleared the temple of money changers and animals (e.g., Matthew 21:12; John 2:14-15). Right now, however, I highlight two instances in the gospel of Mark where Jesus is explicitly described as angry or indignant.[1] The first is in Mark 3:5, which is part of a miracle story.

> Again he entered the synagogue, and a man was there who had a withered hand. They watched him to see whether he would cure him on the sabbath, so that they might accuse him. And he said to the man who had the withered hand, "Come forward." Then he said to them, "Is it lawful to do good or to do harm on the sabbath, to save life or to kill?" But they were silent. He looked around at them with anger; he was grieved at their hardness of heart and said to the man, "Stretch out

your hand." He stretched it out, and his hand was restored. The Pharisees went out and immediately conspired with the Herodians against him, how to destroy him. (Mark 3:1-6)

The onlookers in the story included Jewish religious leaders, as can be discerned from the immediately preceding story (Mark 2:23-28). Those onlookers were more concerned about Jesus violating Sabbath laws than they were about the man with a withered hand. It is common today for religious people to appeal to *law and order* rather than focus on real people and their needs. There are many subjects where this attitude is evident, such as the prison industrial complex, anti-drug legislation, capital punishment, and the reluctance to address police brutality. Another example is our immigration fiasco. Few people are content with the situation, as millions of people flee their homelands with the hopes of starting a new life in the USA or somewhere else. Solutions to the problem are elusive. Conservative voices—including many evangelicals— articulate their fear of people they label as "illegal." The foci of evangelical anger are immigrants of color, not people coming from Northern Europe. Christians who seek to restrict immigration can be heard sarcastically asking, "What part of *illegal* don't you understand?" The law is the ostensible cause of their concern, just as it was for the religious people in this story from Mark's gospel.

Jesus, however, centers the man with the withered hand. Jesus questions the onlookers about the right course of action: doing good versus doing harm, saving life versus killing. The choice should be obvious, so Jesus performs the miracle to make clear that human wholeness is more important than laws—even ones held to be sacred. Just before Jesus heals the man, however, he gets angry with the onlookers. The way that Mark tells the story, it seems that Jesus responds out of his anger. He gets angry, then commands that the man stretch out his hand. Surely Jesus intended to help the man as soon as he saw him in the synagogue, but the healing happens after Jesus expresses his anger.

Jesus grieved the hard-heartedness among the onlookers. The hard-hearted people were more interested in Jesus upholding their traditions than in the man's predicament. With a functional hand, the man, although unnamed, could receive dignity and respect. He would be able to work. He would lose the stigma of having his ailment interpreted as divine disapproval. The man would have an opportunity to flourish. Perhaps it is still the case that Jesus is angry with those who are concerned more with prohibitions than with human flourishing.

Sadly, the story ends with the onlookers developing violent intentions. Members from two groups that did not normally work well together, Herodians and Pharisees, conspire not merely to silence Jesus, but to kill him. Interestingly, we are currently witnessing a conspiracy of two entities that did not always work well together. For years, evangelicals in the USA viewed the government as evil. Evangelicals maintained their distance from society with strategies such as starting their own schools, camps, and neighborhoods. The government was *secular* and consequently, ungodly. However, it has been especially evident since 1976, which *Time* magazine dubbed "the Year of the Evangelical," that evangelicals have conspired with the government, often with candidates making their faith part of their political platform. Evangelicals rely on the government to focus on law and order even when it might thwart human flourishing. In a manner of speaking, it could be that religious people and government forces are conspiring to kill Jesus—or at least the witness of Jesus.

Another episode in Mark's gospel describes Jesus as indignant, a word that is synonymous with angry.

> People were bringing little children to him in order that he might touch them; and the disciples spoke sternly to them. But when Jesus saw this, he was indignant and said to them, "Let the little children come to me; do not stop them; for it is to such as these that the kingdom of God belongs. Truly I tell you, whoever does not receive the kingdom of God as a little child will never enter it." And he took them up in his arms, laid his hands on them, and blessed them. (Mark 10:13-16)

Children held no status in ancient society. Therefore, it's not surprising that the disciples tried to stop people from bringing their children for a touch from Jesus. We tend to want our leaders to engage with important people—those of high status—rather than those who have little or nothing to offer. Jesus developed a reputation for spending quality time with people of low status and ill repute (e.g., Matthew 9:10-11; 11:19; Mark 2:15-17; Luke 5:27-32). When Jesus gets angry because the disciples are rebuking people who bring their children to him, he creates a teachable moment. Jesus commands that the children not be hindered. He picks up the children, places his hands on them, and blesses them. Along with actions that indicate warmth, welcome, and divine favor, Jesus' words connect children to the kingdom of God. The children become the teachers. Children are vulnerable and often trusting, and perhaps Jesus wants to connect entrance into God's kingdom to those who recognize their vulnerability and offer their trust to God. But we must also consider the marginal status of children.

Children represent those who are easily ignored, pushed to the side, and viewed as inconvenient, and whose needs take a backseat to the needs of those considered to be more important. Jesus gets indignant when the weak are marginalized; hopefully we are similarly indignant. Perhaps our anger can give rise to teachable moments for those with ears to hear, when the vulnerable become the teachers.

ANGRY PAUL

I find Jesus' anger liberating because it not only illustrates the point made in the verses at the start of the chapter (Ephesians 4:26-27), but also legitimates my anger against injustice. Jesus, however, is not the only biblical hero who got angry. There are many, like Moses (Exodus 32:19) and David (2 Samuel 12:5). Not all anger, of course, is justified or leads to positive action. However, the apostle Paul is a prominent New Testament figure in addition to Jesus who used anger to prompt positive change. There's no doubt that Paul got angry over certain sinful behaviors, such as sexual immorality or drunkenness (see Galatians 5:19-21). Most Christians I've known would limit Paul's anger to such sins, and would not recognize Paul's anger toward injustice. In fact, there is a story about Paul becoming indignant when his personal rights were violated. That story is especially significant for marginalized people because Christians in the dominant culture oftentimes have either minimized any notion of civil rights for minorities and women or denounced protests designed by the oppressed to assert their civil rights.

Acts 16:6-40 recounts the adventures of Paul and Silas as they evangelized the prominent city of Philippi. The drama of Paul and Silas in Philippi is remarkable, with several characters who stimulate our imaginations, and the extraordinary conversion of a jailer that understandably takes center stage. Yet there is an epilogue that often gets omitted in contemporary storytelling. Acts 16:35-40 describes the end of Paul and Silas's episode in Philippi:

> When morning came, the magistrates sent the police, saying, "Let those men go." And the jailer reported the message to Paul, saying, "The magistrates sent word to let you go; therefore come out now and go in peace." But Paul replied, "They have beaten us in public, uncondemned, men who are Roman citizens, and have thrown us into prison; and now are they going to discharge us in secret? Certainly not! Let them come and take us out themselves." The police reported these words to the magistrates, and they were afraid when they heard that they were Roman citizens; so they came and apologized to them. And they took them out and asked them to leave the city. After leaving the prison they went to Lydia's home; and when they had seen and encouraged the brothers and sisters there, they departed.

Paul, when he heard that he and Silas were free to go in peace, ironically became irritated and remained in the prison. Paul recounted the unjust treatment that he and Silas received, and demanded that the magistrates appear in person. Paul and Silas had their civil rights violated by Roman authorities. As Roman citizens, Paul and Silas should have had a fair trial, not a beating and imprisonment at the urging of a mob (see Acts 22:25). The magistrates were afraid (v. 38) because they realized that they had violated the prisoners' rights. The magistrates did indeed appear in person and apologized, but also urged Paul and Silas to leave the city. Perhaps if Paul and Silas remained in the area, the magistrates would have to face increasing scrutiny for their actions. Paul and Silas apparently did not rush out of the city, as they took time at Lydia's home to minister to the new believers (v. 40).

Paul made a public demand for justice based on his status as a citizen of Rome in the Roman colony of Philippi, one of the most patriotic cities in the empire (Acts 16:12). Being a follower of Jesus did not prevent Paul from appealing to his earthly citizenship to point out injustice. An apology was acceptable to Paul and Silas; they did not seek anything else from the government. In discussing this incident, biblical scholar Willard Swartley suggests that Paul and Silas sought an apology because peace seeks the restoration of relationships—even between citizens and the state, and is possible "only when misdeeds are duly acknowledged."[2] We see in the apostle's protest a parallel to our own. Roman citizenship brought privileges and responsibilities. Those who were not citizens by birth did all they could to become citizens (see Acts 22:28). As a citizen, Paul could appeal to the mighty Roman authorities and expect his voice to be heard.

Mary Beard, professor of classics, asserts that "[Roman] citizenship brought with it all kinds of specific rights under Roman law, covering a wide range of topics, from contracts to punishments. The simple reason that, in the 60s CE, Saint Peter was crucified while Saint Paul enjoyed the privilege of being beheaded was that Paul was a Roman citizen."[3] The mode of execution might not be our first example of what constitutes privilege, but Roman citizenship provided advantages. As far as we know, Paul did not denounce all the various evils within Roman society, such as slavery, or advocate for the reform of the government. However, arguments from silence are meaningless. What is evident from Acts 16:35-40, as well as other places (e.g., Acts 22:22-29), is that Paul could be angry and rely on his Roman citizenship to give him a voice when faced with injustice, such as when he was in the Roman penal system. Notice that Paul's citizenship not only made his evangelistic efforts easier, but also allowed him to advocate for his physical well-being.

ANGER AND SOCIAL CHANGE

It's painful to acknowledge that mass shootings have become commonplace. Along with boasts about the United States' exceptionalism is the horrendous reality that people in our country kill fellow humans at alarming rates. National Public Radio cites research from the University of Washington's Institute for Health Metrics and Evaluation and observes, "The level of gun violence in the United States is completely outsized compared to what's seen in other wealthy countries. In fact, the rate of gun violence in the U.S. is higher than in many low-income countries."[4] After one such episode of gun violence, young people across the country expressed their outrage, which prompted Judith T. Moskowitz, a professor of medical social sciences, to offer observations and commentary on the role of anger in effecting social change:

> Anger, despite its reputation, is not a bad thing. When faced with the repeated tragedy of mass shootings, complex feelings of anger, sadness, fear, and disgust are common, normal, and important to allow, not only for our own well-being, but in order to work towards real and impactful change. . . . We must recognize that we can all benefit from emotions like anger as much as positive emotions like gratitude. In times of stress we need to allow ourselves the full range of emotional experience

and encourage those around us to do the same. Young people who are speaking out and working towards meaningful change in the aftermath of this most recent shooting seem to be doing this very thing, that is, experiencing and expressing a wide array of emotions, encouraging full expression of feelings in those around them, and channeling their emotions into action. The rest of us can learn from them, and allow ourselves to experience the full range of human emotions, then allow them to guide us productively. So let us go ahead and count our blessings, but let's not let that blunt the anger that motivates us to be most engaged in the world.[5]

I've already acknowledged that anger was among the forces that propelled advances in civil rights for African Americans. Angry women have led the charge to dismantle patriarchy.[6] For decades many women exercised faith and fortitude in the fight to be respected as fully human. This has been especially true for women of color whose anger challenged notions of respectability. Black women have had to fight racism as well as sexism. It would be surprising if they were not angry! My daughter-in-law, Dr. Erica Edwards, researches educational policies, particularly those impacting girls and women of color. She points out that black girls often face discipline in school for failing to conform to white people's expectations of what a "good" girl should be, which includes not getting angry. Edwards observes, "When we ask girls to sit on their emotions, to keep silent and pretend as if the school conflict they experience is natural, we reify hegemonic femininity—those violent ideals premised upon the notion of white women's fragility."[7] Edwards, after reflecting on Sojourner Truth's famous "Ain't I a Woman?" speech of 1851, further remarks that "throughout history, Black women's survival depended upon our ability to be more than just 'good.' We have had to fight—physically, emotionally, politically, intellectually, and spiritually—to hold onto ourselves and our people."[8]

As I reflect on the legitimacy of anger, I do not mean to offer a utilitarian perspective where the ends justify the means. Not all anger is redemptive. However, anger can be a powerful motivator to create something good. Theologian James Cone once affirmed a student who angrily challenged him in class by saying, "Your anger is how theology begins. It starts with anger about a great contradiction that can't be ignored."[9]

EXERCISING THE POWER OF ANGER

A few years ago, several members of my family and I stopped watching and otherwise supporting the National Football League. I used to enjoy football, having been the captain of my football team in high school and a player in college for a season. I was a fan of the sport. However, I became disenchanted for a variety of reasons, including the NFL's poor record of acknowledging and dealing with brain injuries that players sustained from multiple concussions, and also the way team owners mistreated quarterback Colin Kaepernick. Kaepernick expressed frustration over police brutality against African Americans and refused to stand for the playing of the national anthem before games. The backlash came from far and wide, including the White House. The president of the United States, Donald Trump, joined with others in misrepresenting Kaepernick's concern, accusing the young athlete—who identifies as African American and Christian—of being unpatriotic and disrespecting the US armed forces. An aspect of the privilege that whiteness brings is the ability to hijack the narrative that accurately tells the story of marginalized people. However, in time, increasing numbers of people will grow in awareness of the truth behind Kaepernick's protest; that happens when angry people keep making noise.

The NFL is a behemoth, so my boycott is meaningless from a financial standpoint. Any boycott of the NFL would have to be astronomically huge to have any deleterious impact on the owners' pocketbooks. The NFL is much bigger than the bus system of Montgomery, Alabama, during the civil rights movement. However, while Kaepernick's anger did not lead to mass boycotts or new legislation, it has affected our society. Kaepernick settled a case against the NFL, suggesting that at least some owners had colluded to keep him out of the league because of his protests. Furthermore, several civil rights organizations honored Kaepernick for taking a stand and losing his job because of that stand.

Anger is a signal that something is not right. You could have a role in making it right. The matters that need correction might be large issues in the world, or they could be much closer to home—something in your church or in your family. Be angry. Then go and do something helpful.

SIX

The Power of Solidarity

Only, live your life in a manner worthy of the gospel of Christ, so that, whether I come and see you or am absent and hear about you, I will know that you are standing firm in one spirit, striving side by side with one mind for the faith of the gospel.

—PHILIPPIANS 1:27

PHILIPPIANS 1:27 IS one of many verses in Philippians that emphasize the apostle Paul's desire for Christian unity. The Christians in Philippi lived in ways analogous to those of Christians in the USA. Philippi was a prominent city and enjoyed the status of being a Roman colony (Acts 16:12). The city took its name from the father of Alexander the Great, Philip II of Macedon. A large percentage of the early inhabitants of the city were veterans, a group most loyal to the empire. There are allusions to Roman imperialism throughout the letter. For example, consider the powerful hymn of 2:6-11 and imagine people who knew what it meant to bow down and hail Caesar as lord. In the hymn, the Christians sing that God's intention is for every knee to bend and every tongue confess that Jesus Christ is Lord (vv. 9-11). In a prominent Roman colony, the Christians were learning to live under the lordship of Jesus, in contrast to the lordship of Caesar. The Philippian believers needed to discern how to live together in light of nationalistic expectations, which is also part of the struggle of Christians in the USA.

The myth that the USA is a Christian nation is fueled, in part, by the generic use of the word *God*, which appears on our currency and is alluded to in our founding documents. However, there is no uniform understanding of *God* among all US citizens. Yet in light of the myth, white evangelicals tend to assume that allegiance to the nation is equivalent to allegiance to God. I once had a seminary student use the word *martyr* to refer to soldiers whose lives were taken in combat. The student insisted that serving one's country in warfare was service for God. It was not clear, however, whether this student would use the term *martyr* for those in another country killed by US forces, even though it is possible that some among those casualties also believed in God. The commingling of nationalism and Christianity contributes to the divisions that exist among Christians in our country. Those divisions have always been present, but have returned to the forefront in recent years. The 2016 election of President Trump, along with the continual support and defense he receives—largely from white evangelicals—serves to highlight divisions among Christians. Of course, there have always been differing political viewpoints among Christians. Yet what concerns many people of color is that some politicians, along with their white evangelical constituents, believe the nation is rooted in a so-called ideal of white supremacy. For some professing Christians, nationalism is more appealing than genuine community rooted in participation in the life of Christ. Like the Philippian Christians, believers in the USA need to be reminded that their citizenship is in heaven (Philippians 3:20).

DIVIDED BY THE GOSPEL

I was able to earn an MDiv with a concentration in urban ministry from Trinity Evangelical Divinity School in Deerfield, Illinois. While taking required courses that examined urban life from a variety of perspectives, I worked at a church on the West Side of Chicago. Over the years, I frequently heard versions of the story of Circle Church, sometimes from professors, but often from the late Glen Kehrein, the founder of Circle Urban Ministries and a former member of Circle Church. Circle Urban Ministries got its name from the community of which it was part as well as from its partnership with Circle Church. The church was an experiment in being an intentionally multiracial church in the 1970s, a time before such churches became fashionable among evangelicals. David Mains was the white pastor, and Clarence Hilliard was the black pastor. The church went through a split, allegedly along racial lines. A frequently mentioned reason for the split was the fallout from the late Rev. Clarence Hilliard's message, whose title betrays its era: "Down with the Honky Christ—Up with the Funky Jesus." Over forty years ago Hilliard made many of the same observations about white evangelicalism that are still being made. For example:

> I said at the outset that we have been preaching a honky Christ to a hungry world. This honky Christ has no content; he does not come to the dispossessed. We preach a honky Christ of easy salvation. Specialists in getting quick, easy decisions for a

strange, mystical, theologically white Christ are rapidly increasing. These persons peddle a Jesus easy to accept, a Jesus who demands very little commitment of energy, money, life. The honky Jesus does not come down from heaven to the lowest social stratum, but he grabs greedily upwards for the good things in life—at least that's the conclusion we could draw if we look at how some of his followers act. I seriously question the nebulous, almost content-less "Lord and Savior Jesus Christ" present in some prominent evangelistic efforts. The Gospel, we are told, means personal salvation and little beyond that. We do not hear about Jesus' uncompromising commitment to liberation from all oppressive, satanic forces.[1]

Prophetic words such as these can alienate those who do not have ears to hear. Preachers like Rev. Hilliard are frequently tagged as angry or radical, and hence are dismissed by white Christians. It has happened to me as well as many colleagues. Over two decades ago, sociologists Michael O. Emerson and Christian Smith pointed out how evangelicalism's individualistic focus makes it virtually impossible for white evangelicals to understand and confront our racist society, much less dismantle it.[2] They write, "From the isolated, individualistic perspective of most white evangelicals and many other Americans, there really is no race problem other than bad interpersonal relationships (or people or programs trying to make it something more than this). And it truly is hard even to think of examples of racism, other than a general sense of bad interpersonal relationships, and occasionally what is heard from the media (if the media can be trusted)."[3]

When prophets like Rev. Hilliard challenge the status quo and upset the dominant culture, they provide the ostensible reason that churches split, or Christian community deteriorates.

However, the true reasons are deeper. Churches built on white supremacy, patriarchy, or the personality of an authoritarian leader cannot tolerate the prophetic voice of the marginalized. The foundation of such communities is tenuous. Christian community must be built upon Christ—his words and his character—and sustained by constant dependence on Jesus. Unfortunately, what passes for Christian community is the fleeting appreciation for a particular preacher, worship style, functional architecture, or children's programming. People gather, but the gathering is not community. Healthy Christian community possesses power to unite people of disparate backgrounds, to build each other up, to contribute to the positive transformation of people and neighborhoods, and to generally demonstrate the reality of a living Lord.

UNITED IN CHRIST

In the verse quoted at the start of this chapter, the expression "live your life in a manner" is a translation of the Greek verb *politeueomai*, which is rare in the New Testament (Acts 23:1 is the only other occurrence). You might be able to observe the word's connection to *polis* and *politics*. *Politeueomai* literally means "I conduct myself as a citizen." Rather than the apostle Paul using his most common verb for behavior, *walk*, he plays on the civic awareness of his readers, encouraging them to take what they understand as good citizenship and apply it to the gospel. Paul indicates that ultimate allegiance is to Christ and his good news, not to the government. Paul reiterates this idea in Philippians 3:20, using a similar word, *politeuma*, often translated as "citizenship." The Philippians, who well understood their civic duty as members of a Roman colony, are actually citizens of a different realm under a different lord. This may have been a challenging realization for those possessing Roman citizenship because such status brought significant privileges. Yielding allegiance to a lord other than Caesar would invite scrutiny and harm. However, for slaves and aliens who did not enjoy the benefits of citizenship, it was good news to be recognized as citizens of the only government that really matters.

Paul expects these heavenly citizens to be "standing firm in one spirit, striving side by side with one mind" (Philippians 1:27). Here there seems to be another allusion to Philippi's rich history. Philip of Macedon, for whom the city was named, developed a fighting technique where soldiers would strive together, fighting side by side as one individual. The phalanx proved to be a powerful military strategy, and Paul encourages the believers to operate in a phalanx of mutual support with regards to the good news of Jesus Christ. There's a meme going around that reads, "If black people could come together like we do for the Electric Slide and Wobble Wobble, we'd be unstoppable." After I stopped laughing, I nodded in agreement. I've officiated many weddings, attended the receptions, and have seen remarkable synchronicity on the dance floor. There is, of course, cohesion among many African Americans, yet we must continue to stay united. Indeed, all people of color must become a phalanx with respect to the gospel, working together side by side. There is power in the unity of marginalized people living and laboring in solidarity.

A recent example of the power present in the solidarity of marginalized people occurred in July 2019. The president of the United States, using his infamous Twitter account, insulted four US congresswomen of color, saying, "Why don't they go back and help fix the totally broken and crime infested places from which they came," even though the president's targets are

US citizens, and three were born in the USA. Representatives Rashida Tlaib, Ayanna Pressley, Ilhan Omar, and Alexandria Ocasio-Cortez—affectionately known as "the Squad"—subsequently gave a press conference. They stood as a phalanx behind the microphone, side by side, visibly supporting one another even though they are of different backgrounds. As people of color who claim allegiance to Christ continue to practice similar solidarity, we demonstrate to the broader society that the gospel of Jesus Christ is authentic and powerful. Our collective voices and actions rebuke the status quo by echoing the voice and actions of a Savior who was also marginalized.

Indigenous peoples as well as those experiencing diaspora—immigrants and African Americans—practice rituals that sustain community cohesion even while enduring pressure from the dominant culture to assimilate. Community cohesion is not bigotry. People of color teach everyone the power of community. True community is not a matter of who must be excluded, as is the case with the Ku Klux Klan and other racist organizations whose identity is based on hatred of those marked as outsiders. Genuine community strengthens bonds among members, but also has room at the table for others, even those who were formerly strangers. Healthy communities practice hospitality, which opens the door and sets a place at the table for the newcomer. In fact, the New Testament Greek word for hospitality is *philoxenia*, literally "friend to a stranger." There is much to learn from people who have forged their sense of community under the heat of racism and bigotry. Diverse Christian churches may be the best context to encourage and stimulate the solidarity of people of color. Yet among every non-white Christian group there are stories not only of how difficult it is to live in the USA in general, but of how white Christians compound the struggle.

Multiethnic churches appear to be the remedy for Christian division; but the dynamics of such churches are more complex than we might realize.

Howard Thurman proved to be ahead of his time when he asserted that multiethnic churches could best model the way of life demonstrated and taught by the Lord Jesus.[4] White evangelicals often appear open and eager for their churches to become multiethnic, but the picture is often one of white congregations with some people with darker skin sprinkled throughout. People of color in the congregation gathering in solidarity might strike white members as threatening. I've witnessed the nervous reactions of white people (and also some of their non-white friends) when people of color wanted to caucus in order to discuss issues relevant to their situation. People of color who meet separately in white-dominated spaces may be viewed by whites as radical and subversive. For this reason, as well as a host of others, diverse congregations must center people of color, not white people.

DIVERSITY IS ABOUT POWER, NOT QUOTAS

As an African American I often speak of a black/white divide in the USA, yet being a native New Yorker has allowed me to have a more expansive view of diversity. I have learned that a snapshot of a Sunday worship service that shows people with different skin tones and facial features, or even a roster with many non-European surnames, does not guarantee that the congregation is experiencing the power and other benefits of diverse Christian community. I've been involved in interracial and multiethnic ministry in the USA for over thirty years and have observed that white evangelicals, along with people of color influenced by white evangelicalism, tend to have a limited perspective of multiethnic ministry. In practice, such ministry is usually taken to apply mainly to the worship services. White evangelicals, with allusions to the well-worn observation made by Dr. Martin Luther King Jr. that eleven on Sunday morning is the most segregated hour of the week, act as if the hard work of racial justice has been accomplished when the Sunday service is not all white. Churches that claim to be diverse, yet function with white male leadership, could reach a numerical quota of non-white people but not necessarily reckon with questions of power and equity. On more than a few occasions I have heard white male leaders claim that their church is "like the United Nations." It seemed that those pastors perceived the United Nations as a white organization with some people of color joining in—because that is how their churches often functioned. I understand the United Nations to consist of member nations that have equal representation. The leaders of churches claiming diversity do not always discuss the distribution of power in their congregations. I hasten to add that even leaders of color trained under white evangelicals may mistake integration for equity.

Dr. King's comments about segregated churches were made on *Meet the Press* on April 17, 1960. The interchange was more like an interrogation than an interview, and went beyond the observation about eleven in the morning. Dr. King was asked if his church in Atlanta had any white members and if he thought the government should require that churches be integrated along with schools and stores. Dr. King responded:

> I think it is one of the tragedies of our nation, one of the shameful tragedies, that eleven o'clock on Sunday morning is one of the most segregated hours, if not the most segregated hours, in Christian America. I definitely think the Christian church

should be integrated, and any church that stands against integration and that has a segregated body is standing against the spirit and the teachings of Jesus Christ, and it fails to be a true witness. But this is something that the Church will have to do itself. I don't think church integration will come through legal processes. I might say that my church is not a segregating church. It's segregated but not segregating. It would welcome white members.[5]

The crucial but overlooked parts of Dr. King's response are the last three sentences about his church being *segregated* but not *segregating*, because it would welcome white members. These sentences point toward the church having a posture of hospitality—welcoming the stranger—not merely granting access. There's a vast difference between genuine hospitality and mere access.

Years ago, my wife and I visited a Baptist church one Sunday in a neighborhood that was unfamiliar to us. The congregation appeared to be all white, and posters for Bob Jones University—a school with an unapologetic history of racial segregation—adorned the bulletin boards in the narthex. Both the adult Sunday school lesson and the sermon that followed during the service focused on supporting the Republican candidate for president as opposed to the "secular humanist." It was clear that the church expected a certain type of attendee—white and Republican, at least. By contrast, a few years ago Mother Emanuel AME Church in South Carolina appeared in national news reports because a young white supremacist, intent on murder, was unwittingly welcomed into the church's midweek prayer gathering. Mother Emanuel practiced hospitality, even though it cost nine people their lives. Mother Emanuel's non-segregating posture was more Christlike than that of the Baptist church my wife and I visited.

Churches claiming to be diverse may fail to welcome new members into the full life of the community, especially its leadership. While many white Christians have claimed that their church is like the United Nations, there are also many people of color who left alleged multiethnic churches because the congregations were functionally white, which is to say that the prevailing ethos reflected the views and preferences of the dominant culture. Sociologist Korie L. Edwards describes how African American leaders in interracial churches often defer to white people because racially integrated churches are successful only "to the extent that they are *first* comfortable places for whites to attend."[6] I will never begrudge a minister or pastor of color the opportunity of serving in a predominately white setting; I have done that on more than one occasion. However, when that person feels compelled to *bleach* themselves (as a friend of mine once put it), subduing a significant part of their ethnic identity for the sake of white people, then the Christian power problem is especially evident.

MY JOURNEY TOWARD DIVERSE CHURCH COMMUNITY

My ministry journey has been circuitous, as are most journeys in life. I grew up in Queens, New York, and when I was around ten years old my father suddenly began taking us children to Sunday school at a small storefront church. My mother typically did not join us, but my father seemed to be going through his own spiritual awakening. He gave up smoking cigarettes and drinking any alcohol, and zealously pursued a relationship with Jesus. The church was an Apostolic, *Jesus only* congregation, espousing a oneness theology. This is to say that the church taught that there was no Trinity; the Lord Jesus Christ is simultaneously the Father, Son, and Holy Ghost. Every sermon concluded with a reference to Acts 2:38, only in the King James Version:

> Then Peter said unto them, Repent, and be baptized every one of you in the name of Jesus Christ for the remission of sins, and ye shall receive the gift of the Holy Ghost.

This verse spelled out the order necessary for personal salvation: repentance, baptism, receipt of the Holy Ghost. Baptism had to be in the name of Jesus, not in the name of the Father, Son, and Holy Ghost (see Matthew 28:19). For my church, there would be a contradiction between Matthew 28:19 and Acts 2:38. The main (actually, only) evidence that someone had received the Holy Ghost was that the person would speak in tongues. This gift of speaking in tongues was not a *second blessing*, as it has been called within charismatic and Pentecostal denominations. In my church, if one did not speak in tongues, that person was not saved.

I had been taught that in order to speak in tongues, I needed to chant "Hallelujah" or "Jesus" repeatedly and quickly until I got tongue-tied. The idea of speaking in tongues was awesome. However, being a kid who loved mathematics and was into science, I was suspicious about equating an amazing gift from God with my own fatigued stammering and stuttering. Over time I began to wonder why God would not simply let me speak in another language without me having to sweat so much on my knees in that little storefront church. Why was it so hard to get saved?

I nervously went off to college four years after my baptism, wondering why God wouldn't save me, even though I had been faithful in church for years, learning Bible verses, staying out of trouble, and showing up more than most others. Working on a chemical engineering degree while playing football my freshman year was hard enough, but the difficulty was compounded by a concern that I was a disappointment to God. I was told that God would save me if I truly repented. Since I hadn't spoken in tongues, it must mean that I had not truly repented. I wasn't sure what particular sins held me back, so I lived with a constant sense of dread, suspecting that I was being disobedient to God, but not sure how.

I attended that church in Queens during the late 1960s and early 1970s, which was the same time that I was affected by efforts to integrate schools in NYC. Being bused to a white part of Queens for elementary school, I saw that the vast majority of my schoolmates lived different lives from those of my family and neighbors. White people generally had better resources and were consistently getting better educations. Consequently, I wanted the kind of education that they were getting. At the urging of friends, I attended Stuyvesant High School, a well-regarded specialized public school that required an entrance exam. I then went off to Cornell University, an Ivy League institution, because several of my white high school friends were looking to go there. Later, after sensing my own call to ministry, I attended Trinity Evangelical Divinity School (TEDS) at the urging of a white pastor. TEDS is a prominent evangelical seminary; consequently, it is overwhelmingly male and white. White evangelical Christianity has long enjoyed a hegemonic status, setting the tone for what Christianity would look like in America. The evangelicals I met mocked my childhood church. They criticized formally uneducated pastors. They assumed storefront churches were lairs for unscrupulous jackleg preachers who preyed on the naive. White evangelicals did not see that they themselves were part of the system that kept many of us—preachers and otherwise—uneducated and relegated to stereotypes. New Testament scholar Love L. Sechrest rightly observes that "racism not only created deep social, economic, and political disparities between blacks and whites, but it also subverted black access to the intellectual tradition and history of the church."[7]

White evangelicalism has had the power to define Christianity but has been spiritually weak for ignoring the power of those on the margins of society. As a young man struggling to find a place in Christian ministry, I wanted to get the best of both the worlds of white evangelicalism and African American church life. Sechrest describes the way racism not only prevented clergy of color from getting formal theological education, as noted above, but also kept Christianity from learning from the various perspectives of its adherents: "At a minimum it can be said that the body of Christ in this country is impoverished because aspects of the transformative effects of the gospel have been preserved in separate segments of the church, each handicapped by the lack of the other."[8] I wanted to glean from my evangelical education so that I could teach the Bible in a more systematic way and expose economically poorer urban communities—which often were largely African American—to more Christian resources. I also wanted to affirm the celebratory worship of the African American church, our strong sense of community, and our passion for justice in our neighborhoods.

In learning to negotiate a world that claimed to desire racial harmony, I was often the only black person in the room, whether that room was in the workplace, church, or school, or somewhere else. God was apparently calling me to be a racial bridge-builder. In my naivete, I decided to work within evangelicalism, but always in an urban context, striving to bring my worlds together. I became a church planter of a multiethnic church in Brooklyn, New York. The idea of a multiethnic church was not as popular back then as it appears to be today, and it was especially difficult to find white people willing to have a person of color as their pastor. I went on to serve an established church on Capitol Hill, then to plant a congregation out of our home in southeast DC (a largely African American neighborhood), and then served an established congregation in north Minneapolis. In every setting, I thought that a diverse community of Christians—racially, culturally, economically, educationally, generationally, and gender-wise—would best represent the presence of Christ in the world. However, I did not always appreciate how difficult it would be to sustain such a community.

HUMILITY IS NECESSARY FOR DIVERSE COMMUNITY

Unity is an essential building block for genuine community, as the apostle Paul demonstrates throughout his writings, including his letter to the Philippians, which I've referenced in this chapter. Joy is commonly considered to be the major theme in Philippians, and it is true that words for joy and rejoicing are frequent in the letter (e.g., 1:4, 18, 25; 2:2, 17, 18, 28, 29; 3:1; 4:1, 4, 10). However, I want to accentuate the significance of unity that is prominent in the letter. Philippians has an affectionate tone throughout, indicating the apostle's emotional connection to the community (e.g., 1:7-8; 2:25-30; 4:10, 15). There are images and admonitions that celebrate and urge unity (e.g., 1:27; 2:1-5; 4:2-3). Paul also employs the vocabulary of sharing, using words such as *koinonia* and its cognates (1:5; 2:1; 3:10; 4:14, 15).

The opening of Philippians 2 presents a radical proposal for unity:

> If then there is any encouragement in Christ, any consolation from love, any sharing in the Spirit, any compassion and sympathy, make my joy complete: be of the same mind, having the same love, being in full accord and of one mind. Do nothing from selfish ambition or conceit, but in humility regard others as better than yourselves. Let each of you look not to your own interests, but to the interests of others. Let the same mind be in you that was in Christ Jesus. (vv. 1-5)

Unity is the source of the apostle's joy, and that unity is based on humility. In the ancient Greco-Roman world, humility was not a virtue. Humility was shameful to people at the time. The ancients interpreted lowliness as a shortcoming, something shameful that should be avoided. New Testament writings do not advocate the kind of lowliness that is demeaning, but the ancient Greco-Romans did not distinguish between humility and unhealthy servility. The contemporary USA is not much different from ancient times in this regard. Our culture is self-centered, and that includes Christians. Our fascination with celebrity leads us to highlight superstars and revere rugged individualism. Yet our society sends mixed messages: on the one hand we say that humility is a virtue, but on the other hand we give our attention to the loudest and proudest. It is not easy to figure out what humility looks like. Paul's description of humility entails considering others as being more important, or better, than oneself. This sounds impossible and downright un-American!

Such humility is critically important for the survival of diverse Christian communities. In our times, the way that the dominant culture can practice humility is to relinquish power in order to learn from the disinherited. When we started a church in Washington, DC, in a predominately African American and impoverished community, many white friends expressed interest in joining the ministry. Some of the original members of the church expressed hesitancy about their involvement. The hesitancy was due in part to concerns that our African American neighbors would not see themselves as having a place in the new church. Another cause for concern was the common experience of many that white people tend to usurp authority, even within diverse groups. There are many books that center white people in the work of racial justice; that is not my goal here. However, the challenge of Philippians 2:1-5 exists for people of color as well as whites. Humility for whites involves relinquishing power and privilege that is part and parcel of their American experience. For people of color, humility entails renouncing violence or unethical retaliation as a means to gain power and influence.

SEVEN

The Power of Worship

I appeal to you therefore, brothers and sisters, by the mercies of God, to present your bodies as a living sacrifice, holy and acceptable to God, which is your spiritual worship. Do not be conformed to this world, but be transformed by the renewing of your minds, so that you may discern what is the will of God—what is good and acceptable and perfect.

—ROMANS 12:1-2

BELIEVE IN POLITICAL ADVOCACY. As noted in chapter 5, anger over injustice prompted activism that helped to create positive changes in our country. Even so, I have friends who belittle political activism. Some of these friends are white and speak from their place of privilege, since their way of life and personhood have never been questioned or seriously threatened by legislation. Those friends opposed to Christian political involvement express legitimate concern about Christian believers affiliating with particular political parties. Christians could forfeit their prophetic role in society in order to gain influence with one party or another. This is the danger of Christian nationalism. Christians on the political left as well as the right face the temptation to use a political party's platform to represent God. I appreciate the concerns of these friends who are skeptical about political activism, because I know people who put not only their energy into activism—which can be great—but also their hope, which can be misguided. Political activism ought not attempt to baptize any particular party or politician's platform as *Christian*. Instead, activism draws attention to government hypocrisy, shines a light on injustice, and amplifies the voices of the marginalized.

In his sermon "A Knock at Midnight," Dr. Martin Luther King Jr. admonishes, "The church must be reminded that it is not the master or the servant of the state, but rather the conscience of the state. It must be the guide and the critic of the state, and never its tool. If the church does not recapture its prophetic zeal, it will become an irrelevant social club without moral or spiritual authority."[1] Political activism, as important as it may be, is not a substitute for human connection with God. Human power, no matter what person or structure wields it, is impotent compared to the power of God. Our power is ultimately to be found not in the creation or reformation of human political structures, but in our connection to God. Worship connects humans with God. When humans connect with God we find meaning in life, even in the face of calamity and ambiguity. Oppressed people have often communicated the meaningfulness of life through art. Music, poetry, dance, painting, sculpture, and other creative endeavors have long expressed human significance and value even during times of suffering. Suffering people offer God the products of their creative imagination, demonstrating faith and hope while suffering unjustly.

SPIRITUALS: SUBVERSIVE SONGS OF HOPE

Consider the worship many African slaves in the New World offered to God. While the slaveowner's brand of Christianity emphasized commands for slaves to obey human masters (e.g., Colossians 3:22), slaves who came to know Jesus trusted the God who sets people free. This God delivered Israelite slaves out of Egypt (Exodus), delivered three young prisoners of war from death in a furnace (Daniel 3), and restored health and possessions for a godly man afflicted for no apparent reason (Job 1:22; 42:10). Enslaved Christians, upon trusting in the God who delivers, developed their own genre of music, the spirituals, used to lament and to express hope as well as to coordinate escapes. Theologian Arthur Sutherland concludes, "The creators of the spirituals knew the biblical narratives, and they knew the importance of ancestors in African religion. Daniel, Moses, and Jacob became not just figures caught in the pages of the past but living and active participants, even protectors, in the present who could be appealed to for survival."[2] In another work, I point out that slave songs "grew out of the dynamic tension of living with faith in God who promises deliverance, while simultaneously experiencing the slave master's whip. . . . Spirituals helped the slaves to affirm that they were not defined by their work; their identity was rooted in a spiritual reality that transcended their present circumstances."[3]

W. E. B. Du Bois wrote a considerable amount about spirituals, which he referred to as "Sorrow Songs." Du Bois made this observation: "Through all the sorrow of the Sorrow Songs there breathes a hope—a faith in the ultimate justice of things. The minor cadences of despair change often to triumph and calm confidence. Sometimes it is faith in life, sometimes a faith in death, sometimes assurance of boundless justice in some fair world beyond. But whichever it is, the meaning is always clear: that sometime, somewhere, men will judge men by their souls and not by their skins."[4] Du Bois goes on to ask, rhetorically, "Is such a hope justified? Do the Sorrow Songs sing true?"[5] Theologian James Cone examines not only the hope that slaves expressed through spirituals, but also the affirmation of freedom that slaves could not find in white Christianity: "The spirituals are songs about black souls, 'stretching out into the outskirts of God's eternity' and affirming the Word that makes you know that you are a human being—no matter what white people say. Through the song, black people were able to affirm that Spirit who was continuous with their existence as free beings; and they created a new style of religious worship. They shouted and they prayed; they preached and they sang, *because they had found something*. They encountered a new reality; a new God not enshrined in white churches and religious gatherings."[6]

The spirituals are evidence of the power of worship. In their worship, through songs and actions, many slaves were communicating that they had a relationship with a Savior who understood them like no one else, and who would mete out justice at some point. Worship was, of course, directed toward God—the only legitimate object of human worship—but also served as witness. Slaves bore witness in their worshiping, testifying of the True Master, who is mighty and just, in contrast to their human masters.

Worship can be protest. It can be subversive. Much of the time worship in many churches across the USA affirms the status quo. The rituals and music, practiced in comfortable settings with elaborate Christian symbols adorning expensive surfaces, communicate satisfaction. Our opulence, along with happy songs to boost our sense of self-worth, communicates that the world is basically okay, even if I have a few personal issues to get in order. But worship in other times and places, especially when offered through the voices and hands of oppressed people, exclaims that the world is not okay. The world must change. God's love and justice demand change. When people who are on a journey with God understand the good news of Jesus, discern problems in the world, join together in solidarity, encompass the lessons of diaspora people, and channel their anger in positive ways, they demonstrate that transformation via faith in God is possible. True worshipers demonstrate how to wait with hope and not fear. True worshipers back up their words with their actions. When people who are devoted to God serve their neighbors, welcome strangers, and advocate for justice, they demonstrate that love for God is more than pious clichés or empty shibboleths. Worship demonstrates that God is real and that God desires for all creation to be whole.

WORSHIP IS A WAY OF LIFE, NOT AN EVENT

I'm often frustrated at how narrowly many Christians define worship. For some it's only what happens in church at a weekend service. And beyond that, some view worship as only that part of the service when singing takes place. I've been part of more worship planning meetings than I can count, and typically some particular number of minutes is designated for *worship*, meaning *singing*. I'm not trying to pick a fight right now with those who help us draw near to God in song. After all, the Scriptures repeatedly depict God's people as singing, and even command God's people to sing (e.g., Colossians 3:16). Furthermore, the Bible encourages events for the purpose of celebrating and learning about God. From the earliest days Christian believers designated time to eat together, an event that included the eucharist. They also served one another, performed and witnessed baptisms, collected money, and so much more. I will say more about formal worship services, but right now I want to stress the point that God has always desired followers whose way of life demonstrated faith and devotion. This is to say that worship has always been more about a way of life than about a particular event.

In the Bible, God speaks through prophets, whose messages included the admonition that God desires people to demonstrate devotion in their lives even more than perform the rituals associated with formal, institutional worship. One of the more frequently quoted passages is from the prophet Amos:

> I hate, I despise your festivals,
>   and I take no delight in your solemn assemblies.
> Even though you offer me your burnt offerings and grain
>   offerings,
>   I will not accept them;
> and the offerings of well-being of your fatted animals
>   I will not look upon.
> Take away from me the noise of your songs;
>   I will not listen to the melody of your harps.
> But let justice roll down like waters,
>   and righteousness like an ever-flowing stream.
>   (Amos 5:21-24)

Over the years, many people, including Dr. King, have quoted that last verse about justice and righteousness. Those concepts describe a way of being rather than an event. In fact, the aspects of formal worship—including the offering of animals and produce as well as musical celebration—are abhorrent to God in the absence of justice and righteousness. Justice and righteousness include attitudes and behaviors that demonstrate love for God and love for other people. Justice and righteousness are to cascade down in torrents like a waterfall.

Another frequently quoted passage is from the prophet Micah, who ministered around the same time as Amos:

> "With what shall I come before the LORD,
>   and bow myself before God on high?
> Shall I come before him with burnt offerings,
>   with calves a year old?
> Will the LORD be pleased with thousands of rams,
>   with ten thousands of rivers of oil?
> Shall I give my firstborn for my transgression,
>   the fruit of my body for the sin of my soul?"
> He has told you, O mortal, what is good;
>   and what does the LORD require of you
> but to do justice, and to love kindness,
>   and to walk humbly with your God? (Micah 6:6-8)

Similar to Amos, Micah urges justice, along with mercy, or kindness, as well as humility along the journey with God. The sacrifices that were part of the formal worship gathering are exaggerated here, emphasizing how little God desires those material things in contrast to justice, kindness, and humility, exercised in a relationship with God. There are many more passages in the Hebrew Bible that make a similar case, especially Isaiah 58. That entire chapter addresses the shortsightedness of viewing corporate, formal gatherings held in God's name as worship when injustice persists. Worship is fundamentally a reorientation of values.

The passage from the opening of Romans 12, cited at the start of the chapter, is one of many in the New Testament that echo the prophets of the Hebrew Bible. According to the apostle Paul, genuine worship entails the offering of our entire selves—bodies and souls. Romans 12:1-2 describes "an embodied sacrifice and worship, a lived theology," according to New Testament scholar Scot McKnight.[7] Worship is not conforming to worldly patterns. In context, *worldly* is contrary to *godly*. This is to say that the way of the world is typically in conflict with God's way. Worship involves new ways of thinking, described as the renewal of minds. Entire books have been and could still be written on worship, but the point at the moment is to see that worship is not restricted to the formal events that happen in a gathering of Christians. That sort of gathering is part of worship, but genuine worship goes beyond that.

The Lord Jesus taught a bit about worship in his interchange with an unnamed woman of Samaria. The event is recorded in John 4:1-30. While his disciples ran an errand for food in the middle of the day, Jesus rested at a well and engaged a woman in conversation. Critical to the story is the fact that Jews hated Samaritans even though their faith grew from the same roots. We are not told why the woman in the story was collecting water during the hottest part of the day. We need not assume she did so to avoid socializing with other women who looked down on her. What becomes clear is that the woman has had a difficult life. She was married five times and was currently living with a man who was not her husband. During much of my life I've heard sermons shaming the woman because of her multiple marriages as well as her current living situation. Sadly, too many contemporary preachers bring their own biases to this text without acknowledging them. The woman in the story may have been widowed or divorced, or both. In that patriarchal world, women had few rights, and life could be unbearable without a man to protect and provide. Rather than viewing the woman as especially sinful, we would do well to see how she may have been a victim of circumstances.

There are many important points that could be developed from this story, but my focus at the moment comes from verses 19-24:

> The woman said to him, "Sir, I see that you are a prophet. Our ancestors worshiped on this mountain, but you say that the place where people must worship is in Jerusalem." Jesus said to her, "Woman, believe me, the hour is coming when you will worship the Father neither on this mountain nor in Jerusalem. You worship what you do not know; we worship what we know, for salvation is from the Jews. But the hour is coming, and is now here, when the true worshipers will worship the Father in spirit and truth, for the Father seeks such as these to worship him. God is spirit, and those who worship him must worship in spirit and truth."

In response to the woman's curiosity about the location of worship, Jesus goes on to describe how worship is fundamentally about his presence ("the hour is coming, and is now here"). Worship is also about seeking, or pursuing, God spiritually and truthfully. Location is not really an issue, indicating that the formal gathering is not of primary importance. Worship is about following Jesus in order to understand and practice love for God and love for other people.

Since worship is about following the Lord, it would be tempting to try to quantify all that it means to be a follower. Various passages in the Bible command the followers of Jesus to be holy, and we often attempt to define holiness by listing prohibitions (e.g., no smoking, no drinking alcohol, no pre- or extramarital sexual relations, no lying), or perhaps by offering the Ten Commandments as a summary. Holiness should be viewed qualitatively, not quantitatively. This is to say that rather than trying to enumerate an exhaustive list of dos and don'ts—a quantitative approach—it might be better to consider whether one's life is oriented around Jesus. If our allegiance is to Jesus, our attitudes and behaviors cannot help but be affected, and the specifics will depend on our context as well as our individual personalities.

Worship is not about the particular church we attend, or even about our understanding of and adherence to particular doctrinal positions. Worship is about moving in the right direction—along the path that Jesus paved. Following the Lord may lead to clarity in our beliefs as well as adjustments to our behavior, but worship doesn't start with those things. It starts with faith in Jesus as king and a commitment to obey and follow. Such commitment requires a reorientation of our lives.

WORSHIP AS WITNESS

One Wednesday evening when I was leading a Bible study at the church I served in Minneapolis, a man wandered into the building for the first time shortly before our meeting was to start. The construction of our church's meeting space had recently been completed, so we were still new to gathering there for our weekly study. The man happened to see people entering the building, so he came in and started to look around. None of our group seemed to notice him, but I did, so I went over and introduced myself—not as the pastor; just with my first name. In turn, he introduced himself to me. I'll call him Derrick, but that's not his real name. I offered to give Derrick a tour of our new facility, and he appreciated that. Derrick asked a bunch of questions about the church, as he had witnessed the building's construction over the past several months. He said he would not stay for Bible study, but he actually ended up doing so. In fact, he came back the next week, and all the weeks after, up until the time I moved from serving that church.

Derrick eventually told me that he stayed because he was impressed, not with any particular lesson in the study, but with the people who came. He noted how some volunteered food to share. Others demonstrated vulnerability as they shared personal stories. Derrick was surprised to find that I was the senior pastor because I did not fit his stereotype of a pastor—a stereotype shaped by his previous church experiences. During my time with Derrick I watched him open his heart to God. He acknowledged past pains inflicted by churches, by white people, and by others who had some authority over his life. But when he stumbled upon our gathering, he committed himself to Jesus and to not give up on trying to be the man God would want him to be. Even though I would love to see the people of God work to make large, sweeping changes in society, I simultaneously celebrate and encourage the witness that worshipers have in seemingly smaller ways—including the witness shown to one solitary individual.

When we understand worship to be a way of life rather than an event, it will influence our entire way of being. I recycle used items because as a worshiper of God I want to steward the resources of the planet as best I can. Recycling and driving my hybrid car are small things that I hope can lead to greater things. I have seen worshipers in the USA, as well as in the few other countries I've been able to visit, give money and time generously, practice hospitality joyfully, relate to their spouses and children respectfully, and otherwise represent Jesus outside the four walls of a church building. That type of witness has power.

GATHERING TOGETHER

In this chapter I purposely tried to give more attention to worship outside a building, or apart from some formal gathering, but I also consider what happens among a group of worshipers to be important. I've had people tell me that they don't need church; they can worship God in nature. When it comes to the question of formal gatherings versus private reflection in natural settings, I don't understand worship to be an *either-or* but a *both-and* matter. This is to say that when worship is a way of life, there is a rhythm that incorporates formal gatherings as well as private times of solitude and meditation. The people of God need to meet together (see Hebrews 10:25). We need to eat together. We need to take communion together, baptize new believers together, pool our money together, and serve our neighbors together. Yet even as I list those particular activities, I'm not trying to describe what worship gatherings should look like. I simply want to encourage us to worship God wholeheartedly.

Right after seminary I planted a church in Brooklyn, New York, called New Community, which I mentioned in earlier chapters. When I graduated, I had the permission from a denomination to plant a church, but there was no plan for financing. Church planting in those days was not always as strategic as it has become in many circles today. Consequently, I scrambled to find a job but did not secure one upon graduation. Just when money dried up, as we were living on the kindness of others, I managed to gain a position at a private school, teaching mathematics, and eventually also chemistry. There are many stories I could share about that challenging and exhilarating time of life, but at this point I focus on one incident related to worship.

As our young fellowship decided to expand from a Bible study gathering in our tiny apartment in order to include more formal worship services in a rented facility, one woman—I'll call her Jackie (not her real name)—decided to leave the group. Jackie had been consistent for months. I had helped haul her furniture when she moved into an apartment, and others had become friends with her. When I asked her why she was leaving she said, "Church is something that I go to, not something that I'm part of." I will never forget her words. Of course, I knew that people thought that way, but I was naive at the time and didn't think anyone in *our* group would think that way! Ironically, a few weeks later, Jackie called me. She was sick and hoped that my wife, Susan, could pick up a prescription and help with some chores. I was flabbergasted! We had small children at the time, and I didn't believe Susan should make herself available. But Susan felt otherwise, and while I watched our kids in the evening after work, she went out to help Jackie. I was not able to convince Jackie that she was experiencing, through my wife, the very thing she rejected. Jackie needed help and got it from someone who understood what Jackie refused to see. The church is a community of worshipers, so it requires that we be part of a movement and not just attend an event. Jackie was willing to make use of the church, but not to be part of it.

Gathering together with other followers of Jesus is part of what it means to be a worshiper. Oftentimes it is immigrant Christians, as well as believers from otherwise marginalized communities, who best demonstrate the power of corporate worship. As one white friend said to me after attending some predominately African American churches, "White people go to church, but black people *have* church!" That friend had experienced African American churches where people were free to bring their whole selves to the corporate worship experience. But there is a temptation at this point to propagate stereotypes. It is false to conclude that all African American churches have highly emotional services approaching something like the scene in *The Blues Brothers* where Jake and Elwood come to believe that they're on a mission from God. Black churches are not monolithic. I've attended many churches over the years, ranging from liturgical Anglican ones in Rwanda to jumping and shouting white charismatic ones in rural West Virginia. Not all white people of European descent worship like those pictured on *The Simpsons*, where most of the residents of the mythical Springfield worship with constrained emotions and dull repetition, straining to stay awake while listening to Reverend Lovejoy's monotonous droning. Some white people worship like that, but not all. And not all black people worship for three hours, jumping and shouting with pastors whooping and hollering. Some do, but not all. I'm not much concerned about style. But I am sure that church should be something I'm part of, and not just something I go to.

EIGHT

The Power of Hope

For in hope we were saved. Now hope that is seen is not hope. For who hopes for what is seen? But if we hope for what we do not see, we wait for it with patience.

—ROMANS 8:24-25

HOPE GIVES PEOPLE who appear powerless the wherewithal to survive and, in many cases, to thrive. Hope propels people with disabilities whose bodies struggle in environments not designed for them. Hope nourishes people whose poverty makes life bitter in a world dominated by greed. Hope brightens those whose gender prompts others to force them into the shadows. Hope elevates those who've been degraded by whites because of race. Hope is akin to faith in that hope is the confident expectation of a good outcome, as faith is assurance rooted in the character of God (Hebrews 11:1). Without hope, life loses meaning. In his poem "Harlem," also known as "A Dream Deferred," Langston Hughes asks what happens to a dream that is put off, delayed, denied. The poem wonders if such a dream withers away, festers, or turns to rot. In the final line, Hughes wonders if it explodes.[1]

Hughes graphically conveys a sentiment also expressed in some wisdom literature of the Hebrew Bible. For example, "Hope deferred makes the heart sick, but a desire fulfilled is a tree of life" (Proverbs 13:12). Hope, the confident expectation of a good outcome, is present within the migrant traversing treacherous terrain toward an unknown future. Parents who sacrifice to send their kids to college have hope that their children will gain more tools to positively transform society. When we plant trees, recycle, limit pollution, and otherwise care for the environment, we exercise hope that our children's children will have a healthier world in which to live. However, to experience the full power of hope, it must be accompanied by faith in God, the ultimate source of hope.

Spirituals, sung by slaves and their descendants, contain elements of hope. Hope is powerful. Hope propels us to tackle the vicissitudes of life, knowing that there is more to our existence than meets the eye. This is to say that God has greater things in store for his faithful followers than what we experience in this life. Critics of Christianity have complained of its affirmation of an afterlife. These critics have accused Christianity of being a "pie in the sky when you die" religion. They also say that Christians are "so heavenly minded they're no earthly good." Surely those criticisms have been warranted at different times and among different groups. When Christians disregard injustice, show disdain toward immigrants, and reject pleas to care for the environment, all while singing about enjoying heaven's glories, then they are being shortsighted and of no earthly good. When Christians casually spout platitudes to people who've lost loved ones in death, or have suffered injustice, they suggest that Jesus has nothing for people in the present. Apparently, only when the world has ended can there be even a taste of satisfaction.

During the heat of the civil rights movement, Dr. Martin Luther King Jr. offered a "testament of hope" in which he urged hope to be placed in America's ability to do the right thing: "The question that now faces us is whether we can turn the Negro's disillusionment and bitterness into hope and faith in the essential goodness of the American system. If we don't, our society will crumble." King went on to say, "It is a paradox that those Negroes who have given up on America are doing more to improve it than are its professional patriots."[2] Oppressed people, according to King, operate with hope by striving for good within the very society that has alienated them. Part of the strategy of the civil rights movement was to shame the USA into living up to its expressed values of equality for all people.

Having hope for the future entails the belief that at the end of time Jesus will reign supreme, having subdued all enemies (1 Corinthians 15:22; Ephesians 1:22; Hebrews 2:8). Yet there can be hope in the present time that God's justice will prevail as a "foretaste of glory divine," to borrow from Fanny Crosby's old hymn, "Blessed Assurance." After all, we pray regularly to God, "Your kingdom come. Your will be done, on earth as it is in heaven" (Matthew 6:10). Dr. King had hope for the future as well as hope in the present. King's ultimate hope was in God, expressed powerfully in his now famous final message that was delivered at Bishop Charles Mason Temple in Memphis, Tennessee, on the eve of his assassination. King likened the civil rights struggle to Israel's journey to the Promised Land, and seemed to have a premonition of his imminent death. In a verbal crescendo, King exclaimed, "But it really doesn't matter with me now, because I've been to the mountaintop. . . . I've seen the Promised Land. I may not get there with you. But I want you to know tonight, that we, as a people, will get to the Promised Land."[3] The sermon illustrates the nature of King's ministry, in which he continually expressed hope for an eternal future with God, but also expressed hope that in his present time, under the power of God, the USA would act justly regarding racism, poverty, and militarism. Hope has both a present and a future dimension, and there is power when we exercise hope.

HOPE IN THE PRESENT

While I was writing this book, one of my sons, along with his wife and infant son, experienced a horrible car accident. Without elaborating on the details, I will say that my family, as well as my daughter-in-law's family and countless friends, exercised the power of hope in God. Hundreds of people—maybe more—cried out to God in faith with hope. While we naturally wonder why God allows such tragedy in the first place, we simultaneously plead to God with hope for change—change in our dispositions as well as positive change in the circumstances. I can say that our families are currently on a healthy trajectory, by the grace of God. Many of our hopes have been realized. The accident was a reminder for me of many things, and one is that we do not truly understand hope until we experience suffering. An affluent teenager in some bedroom community within the USA, hoping for a Lexus on her birthday, is not our best teacher. But her counterpart, suffering in a developing part of the world, praying for clean water and her next meal, is truly our guide for what hope entails.

The power of hope is evident in those who endure suffering. The power is not one-dimensional, but multifaceted. The power, as noted, does involve the ability to teach others, and it also involves the ability to see God in fresh ways. Professors Sylvia C. Keesmaat and Brian J. Walsh, in their exploration of the book of Romans, address the connection between suffering and hope, claiming, "Lament is an act of hope. In fact, it is an act of 'passionate expectation.'"[4] The authors go on to assert, "Hope is always born of lament."[5] Lament is the product of pain and suffering, which gives birth to hope.

The New Testament letter from James offers Old Testament characters, namely the prophets and Job, as examples of people who had hope amid frightful circumstances. Hope reveals itself as patient endurance through suffering: "As an example of suffering and patience, beloved, take the prophets who spoke in the name of the Lord. Indeed, we call blessed those who showed endurance. You have heard of the endurance of Job, and you have seen the purpose of the Lord, how the Lord is compassionate and merciful" (James 5:10-11). We can have hope that we'll experience the Lord's compassion and mercy in the present, not just in the afterlife.

Job is a complex example. The book of Job, named for the main character, is forty-two chapters long. Chapters are somewhat arbitrary divisions, as they were not part of the original text. Consequently, the number of chapters might not indicate much, as each chapter could be relatively short. But with Job, the chapters themselves are long, and the total number is greater than most other books of the Bible. Despite Job's great length, we tend to reduce the story to a few parts from the beginning, perhaps with a small bit of the middle, and then a brief mention of the end. The basic story of Job that we tell is that God brags on Job to Satan (Job 1:8), and God allows Satan to attack Job with horrible afflictions, including sickness, loss of children, and loss of wealth (Job 1:12; 2:4). Job's wife urges him to "curse God, and die" (Job 2:9), while some of his associates visit, but do a poor job of encouraging Job. Yet after some time, God rewards Job with the restoration of his fortune and with new children (Job 42). We typically aren't sure what to make of all the long speeches between the beginning and ending of the book of Job. Consequently, the story of Job comes off like a fairy tale where the hero lives "happily ever after." While I continue to try to make sense of the whole book of Job, at this point I can point out a couple of things that relate to the topic of hope: (1) Job's situation was not about punishment, and (2) Job expected justice.

The ordinary view of God's justice is "eye for eye" and "tooth for tooth," a tit-for-tat payback system (see Deuteronomy 19:21). An idea that emerges from this view of divine justice is that we get what we deserve. Our suffering is taken to be the result of our personal sinful actions. In Job's story, one of the men who came to sit with him in his grief, Eliphaz the Temanite, expresses conventional wisdom around suffering, that good people don't suffer (Job 4:6-7). Our culture often blames victims for their suffering. People hamstrung by poverty are labeled as lazy. Addicts struggling to be healthy in mind and body are viewed as weak. Ethnic minorities who face discrimination are dismissed for failing to show proper respect or deference to the systems already in place. We see this every time a black or brown body is harassed or killed by police. Immediately after the altercation, the victim's background—every unsavory detail—is put on public display, even if it has absolutely nothing to do with their victimization.

In the gospel of John, there's a story about Jesus healing a man who was "blind from birth" (John 9:1). The disciples of

Jesus asked, "Rabbi, who sinned, this man or his parents, that he was born blind?" (John 9:2). As in modern times, people in ancient times tended to blame victims for their suffering. Jesus answered his disciples, saying, "Neither this man nor his parents sinned; he was born blind so that God's works might be revealed in him" (John 9:3). Suffering is not indicative of God's punishment. It can instead be an occasion for hope, for God to demonstrate mighty power.

The book of Job wrestles with *theodicy*, the question of why a good God allows bad things to happen, especially to those we deem to be innocent. Rather than blaming the victims of suffering, we do well to recognize that there are no simple answers. Sin has been active in the world since the earliest days. The book of Genesis does not dwell on the origins of evil, but illustrates the results of evil: death and destruction. Humans enslaved and victimized by sin need to be delivered, not blamed. Those who fail to accept God's deliverance may reap the consequences of their rejection, but those who suffer are not always the ones to blame. In the book of Job, the blame goes to Satan. The book makes evident that Job was not responsible for his plight, as he was "blameless and upright, one who feared God and turned away from evil" (Job 1:1).

Job's suffering was not about punishment, and Job hoped for vindication—even in his lifetime. In the midst of his pain, Job replies to another companion, Bildad the Shuhite (Job 18:1; 19:1). Throughout Job 19, frustration pours from our protagonist, directed toward his companions but also toward God. Job starts by asking his companions, "How long will you torment me, and break me in pieces with words?" (Job 19:2). He goes on with his recriminations and voices this accusation against God: "Know then that God has put me in the wrong, and closed his net around me" (Job 19:6). After Job recounts all his charges against God, a litany of his travails, he exclaims,

> For I know that my Redeemer lives,
>   and that at the last he will stand upon the earth;
> and after my skin has been thus destroyed,
>   then in my flesh I shall see God,
> whom I shall see on my side,
>   and my eyes shall behold, and not another.
>   My heart faints within me! (Job 19:25-27)

Job's words express hope. But in whom does Job have hope? Many Bible readers understand *redeemer* to be God; notice the NRSV's uppercase *R*. Some people even go so far as to conclude that Job has in mind the New Testament teaching of the final resurrection, with Jesus as Redeemer. However, other scholars see the redeemer as someone other than God. The Hebrew *go'el* (*redeemer*) was a legal term and could apply to one who avenges the murder of a family member (see Numbers 35:19; Deuteronomy 19:6). Job has hope that justice will prevail, and someone will demonstrate—to God and to onlookers—that Job has done nothing wrong to deserve his pain and suffering. The destruction of Job's skin (v. 26) is not necessarily a reference to his death. While some scholars have argued that the destruction of Job's skin is a reference to his death, others believe that it is not a metaphor for death.

The book's poetry suggests that Job sees his physical agony, accompanied by the scraping of his flesh (Job 2:8), as deterioration of his skin, not his death.[6] Job expects that in his lifetime his redeemer will plead his case in God's courtroom.[7]

The book of Job challenges our cause-and-effect view of justice, where people simply get what they deserve. Job's words teach us, at least in part, that anyone—even an upright person—can suffer. We also learn that people who suffer, who face injustice and get the short end of life's stick, can still have hope. Even when we are angry with God, as Job was, or as some of my family was after the car accident, we can recognize that we are not always to blame for our suffering, and that God's justice means our eventual vindication.

HOPE FOR THE FUTURE

An important feature of hope is its ability to help us see beyond our present circumstances. But that view of the future must go beyond the near future to include a glimpse of eternity. Part of our human existence is knowing that injustice will not cease until the world comes to an end. We will likely pass from the scene before all things are made right in the world. Ultimate justice can come only when the Lord Jesus Christ returns and wraps up human history. Consequently, our hope cannot rest in other humans, or in human structures. Only God can make humanity's future secure.

Advocacy is good, as I've mentioned earlier. Some gains are won through public protest, some through prophetic words, and some at the ballot box. However, there are those, including some of my friends, who downplay the value of voting. These friends view voting as putting too much hope in human institutions. Judging from the time and energy that some people— even Christians—put into supporting particular candidates, I agree that we might conclude that too much is being expected from politicians. Yet there is no question that some political officials have championed the cause of the weak and marginalized. People who have fought for civil rights and human rights in the USA and around the world do not take the privilege of voting for granted. I am continually amazed at the fact that it was during my childhood that voting rights legislation passed, outlawing discriminatory practices. Voting rights for women and minorities in the USA is not ancient history. Those with social hegemony have the privilege of dismissing the significance of voting. However, it is possible to appreciate the power of making changes in society without putting all our hopes in human institutions.

Change is going to come. God will rebuild the creation. That message reverberates throughout the Scriptures. When Israel's prophets announced the *day of the LORD*, they had in mind some future time—not a twenty-four-hour period, but an event—when God would judge evildoers and vindicate God's followers. Isaiah 13:6; Jeremiah 46:10; Ezekiel 30:3; and Joel 1:15 are a few of the many places in the Old Testament that describe the day of the LORD. The day of the LORD indicates the time when God will visit humanity in an exceptionally powerful manner. God's visit will be doomy and gloomy for those opposed to God, but gratifying for those harassed by God's enemies. Prophecies of the day of the LORD served as warnings to those who rebelled against God, but also as promises of ultimate deliverance for the people of God. In fact, on the day of Pentecost, when the Holy Spirit comes to empower and indwell the earliest disciples of Jesus (Acts 2:1-4), the apostle Peter arises to preach, and quotes the prophet Joel concerning the day of the LORD (Acts 2:14-20).

New Testament writers saw the coming of the Holy Spirit and the return of Jesus Christ as consonant with the Old Testament day of the LORD. In fact, the apostle Paul uses "day of the Lord" and "day of Christ" interchangeably (e.g., 1 Thessalonians 5:2; 2 Thessalonians 2:2). The New Testament affirms that with the return of Jesus, all will be made as it should be. We call the return of Jesus the second coming. The New Testament refers to the return of Jesus as the *Parousia* (Greek for "presence" or "coming"), such as in Matthew 24:3; 1 Corinthians 15:23; 1 Thessalonians 2:19; 3:13; and 4:15. Believers in Jesus are to have hope in the *Parousia* (see James 5:7-8). In Titus 2:13, Paul explicitly connects hope to the appearance of Jesus: "While we wait for the blessed hope and the manifestation of the glory of our great God and Savior, Jesus Christ."

The resurrection of believers accompanies the return of Jesus (e.g., 1 Corinthians 15:50-54; 1 Thessalonians 4:16-17). Followers of Jesus live with the hope that what is dead will be brought to new life. The entire creation, being "subjected to futility" (Romans 8:20), "waits with eager longing" (v. 19). Resurrection means a brand-new existence where, as the old folks used to say, "the wicked will cease from troubling and the weary will be at rest." Resurrection means a world devoid of sin, injustice, sickness, and death (Revelation 21:1-8). Having hope in the resurrection is not a cop-out; nor does it excuse us from addressing the various injustices in our world. In fact, hope in the resurrection should push us to work even harder to right the wrongs of the world. If God has a better world in view for humanity, then God's people should help others see a glimpse of that world. The followers of Jesus, by embodying the gospel, demonstrate God's intentions for the world. Our lament over the conditions of the world should push us toward attitudes and actions that anticipate resurrection.

Christians who advocate for social change are heralding the resurrection. They are announcing the good news of the kingdom of God. The kingdom of God means new life, and the *Parousia* is when that kingdom is fully realized and all things are made new. Sadly, Christian advocates of social justice have been accused of "rearranging the deck chairs on the *Titanic*." In other words, working to dismantle racism, to alleviate suffering, and to champion the cause of the oppressed is meaningless since the world will come to a violent end. This attitude may be why many evangelicals deny the reality of climate change or, if they accept climate change, deny that humans contribute to it. These evangelicals reckon that if the world is headed to a chaotic, fiery end (see 2 Peter 3:12), then it does not make sense to work against the entropic forces of destruction.

My wife and I once attended a church for a while that was overwhelmingly white and where we were the only African Americans who attended regularly. For a variety of reasons related to our circumstances, as well as our attempts to discern a call God was placing on our lives, we stayed at the church for about two years prior to my attending seminary. There was a time at that church when the pastor created opportunities for listeners to ask questions after his evening messages (it was in the days when Sunday evening services in addition to morning services were common). The pastor had preached on Paul's instructions to Timothy in 1 Timothy 5:3-16 about the treatment of widows. After the sermon, during the Q&A, I asked what our church could do to address inequities in society. The first thing the pastor said in his response was, "We need to preach the gospel!" He got rousing responses of "Amen!" I felt small for suggesting that we could care for people in practical ways. After all, it seemed that Paul was giving Timothy practical instructions for the care of vulnerable women in his time. The irony is that the church where I had asked that question had, many years earlier, created a care facility for the elderly. It had started out serving members of that church community, who were primarily Northern European immigrants, but over the years cared for a variety of people. Somewhere in that church's history people felt the need to create a ministry for the vulnerable senior population. Yet they did not come to see that as an act of social justice.

Acts of mercy and justice display hope in the resurrection. Dr. Rebecca Crumpler, the first African American woman to earn an MD degree, specialized in caring for women, children, and the poor—the most vulnerable members of society. Dr. Crumpler also authored a textbook, *A Book of Medical Discourses in Two Parts*, published in 1883. Dr. Crumpler defied the odds, which were seriously stacked against her, to bring wholeness to other marginalized people. Such is the work rooted in resurrection hope. Resurrection hope expresses itself in confidence that God's kingdom will come in fullness at the end of time. When the Lord Jesus miraculously healed people during his time on earth, he was demonstrating that the kingdom of God was present. When he sent his disciples on a mission, the Lord connected their ministry of healing with the kingdom of God: "Cure the sick who are there, and say to them, 'The kingdom of God has come near to you'" (Luke 10:9). The kingdom of God is dynamic, moving throughout the world, advancing toward a climactic fulfillment. The gospel message is about the nearness of the kingdom (Mark 1:15). Hope in the resurrection is part of the gospel's message. Consequently, the work of social justice anticipates God's ultimate good work, which reaches fruition at the return of Jesus.

Sylvia Keesmaat and Brian Walsh reflect on the passage that opened this chapter, Romans 8:24-25, and claim, "It is in the tension between what is seen and unseen between the undeniably painful reality in which we live and the vision of a coming restoration of all things that hope is born."[8] I've mentioned that prophets denounce injustice and invite people to repent. Prophets also help give meaning to the tension between what is seen and what is unseen. They communicate that the world is not as it should be, but they give us hope by pointing to God, the one who restores and renews. Hope provokes our imaginations, allowing us to envision a world where God's justice reigns. It is in our painful reality, as Keesmaat and Walsh admit, that hope emerges, causing us to yearn for restoration. Those who experience life's pain often have the most vivid picture of what restoration looks like. Their hope not only sustains them, but propels them onward. There is indeed power in hope, and oftentimes those on the margins of society who have faith in Jesus best demonstrate that hope.

The Power of the Spirit

*Take the helmet of salvation, and the sword of the Spirit,
which is the word of God. Pray in the Spirit at all times
in every prayer and supplication. To that end keep alert
and always persevere in supplication for all the saints.*

—EPHESIANS 6:17-18

EVIL IS AT WORK in people who hate. But evil is also at work in those who do not hate but are complacent in the face of injustice. Well-meaning people can participate in racism, ableism, patriarchy, nationalism, and a host of other dehumanizing activities. Kind, neighborly people can prop up unjust systems. Fair-minded individuals, churchgoing people, and tax-paying citizens can join with Satan and his demons to corrupt God's work in the world. All humanity is stained by sin. Because *evil* might be an abstraction for us, we want to put faces and names to evil. It is easier to blame particular people for injustice than to see entire institutions, systems, and even governments as corrupt. There has been no shortage of despicable characters throughout history who exploited their power and position, even to the point of implementing genocidal policies. Yet evil is not always so obvious. Evil does not always wear a hood. Robin DiAngelo challenges the notion that our understanding of racism should be confined to the actions of people we label as "bad," or to groups like the KKK. D'Angelo challenges the "good/bad binary," in which "racists were mean, ignorant, old, uneducated, Southern whites," but "nice people, well-intended people, open-minded middle-class people, people raised in the 'enlightened North', could not be racist."[1] Racism is an example of a system powered by the spirit of the antichrist. People might willingly or unwittingly participate in that system. In the first century CE, the New Testament author of 1 John declares that the spirit of the antichrist is already at work in the world (1 John 4:3). Whenever people marginalize other human beings, they are allied with potent antichrist agents. These demonic entities endeavor to undermine the work of God in the world.

Evil spiritual forces are at work in the world through people and human institutions. I opened this chapter with Ephesians 6:17-18, which follows from the assertion that "our struggle is not against enemies of blood and flesh, but against the rulers, against the authorities, against the cosmic powers of this present darkness, against the spiritual forces of evil in the heavenly places" (6:12). This pronouncement is especially poignant if the apostle Paul indeed wrote these words to Christians in Ephesus (there is scholarly debate around both issues of authorship and the identity of the recipients of the letter). Ancient Ephesus was known for its religious practices, including occultism. The cult of the Greek fertility goddess Artemis (Diana to the Romans) had a stronghold in Ephesus. In that city stood the temple of Artemis—one of the Seven Wonders of the Ancient World.

Acts 19 describes some of the experiences of the apostle Paul and his ministry partners in Ephesus, highlighting the spiritual conflict between God's messengers and Satan's minions. For example, Paul performs exorcisms, which agitates those who made money from the sale of Artemis artifacts (Acts 19:11-16, 23-29). Despite the opposition that Paul and his coworkers faced, many people became followers of Jesus, some of whom had engaged in occult practices. "Many of those who became believers confessed and disclosed their practices. A number of those who practiced magic collected their books and burned them publicly; when the value of these books was calculated, it was found to come to fifty thousand silver coins. So the word of the Lord grew mightily and prevailed" (Acts 19:18-20). The Christians of Ephesus believed in the power of the spiritual realm. They could testify that followers of Jesus face a supernatural struggle.

The Bible presents demonic forces as real even if we cannot see them. The evil forces—rulers, authorities, cosmic powers, and spiritual forces of evil—are spiritual beings bent on our destruction. These entities, though spiritual, make a tangible impact on the physical world. Satan is connected to these spiritual forces of evil. We meet Satan in both the Old and New Testaments of the Bible. *Satan* means "adversary." One strategy of Satan, the adversary, is to divide and conquer. The adversary provokes human beings to struggle against each other rather than serve each other with love. Such was the case at the very start of the Bible's story. Cain, the firstborn of Adam and Eve, kills his own brother, Abel (Genesis 4:8). Even though Satan is not mentioned in the story of Cain's murder of Abel, the New Testament makes the connection: "We must not be like Cain who was from the evil one and murdered his brother" (1 John

3:12a). "The evil one" is a reference to Satan. The Bible demonstrates that Satan consistently operates contrary to God's will, even catalyzing the sinful tendencies of humans.

All forms of animosity between humans are evidence of demonic work in the world. Humans participate in the evil animated by spiritual entities. As I noted in the opening chapter, we are both victims and perpetrators of sin. Sin enslaves humans so that our attitudes and actions are contrary to God's. Even after we place our faith in Jesus and are liberated from sin, we must actualize that freedom. We need to behave as free people (Romans 6:11-14). When it comes to injustice, it is important to understand that even though humans are complicit in evil, humans are not the enemy. They are tools. In a way, those who sin against others are themselves Satan's victims. Evildoers have fallen for the lies of the "father of lies"—the name Jesus gives to the devil (John 8:44). Satan, our enemy as well as God's, is a predator: "Discipline yourselves, keep alert. Like a roaring lion your adversary the devil prowls around, looking for someone to devour" (1 Peter 5:8).

OUR BATTLE IS SPIRITUAL

The Bible does not explain the origins of evil.[2] However, Scripture readily elaborates on the horrendous impact of evil. The Bible does not glorify sin, but neither does it shy away from presenting its ugliness. Sin infiltrates all of creation and manifests itself in manifold ways. All of creation—humans, animals, and everything else—is touched by sin. As noted in the opening chapter, salvation is about deliverance because humans need to be liberated from sin. Yet humans are not hapless victims of circumstance. At some point we must recognize our complicity with sin. This is part of what repentance entails.

Truly repentant people are intentional about renouncing evil and striving to follow Jesus. In some denominations, when people get baptized (or when they bring their infants for baptism), they agree to renounce Satan, all his works, and all the spiritual forces of wickedness that rebel against God. Although Satan and other demons are at work in the world, we cannot ignore our involvement. We must, in word and action, renounce the works of the devil.

People of my generation may recall the comedian Flip Wilson, one of few African American entertainers of the 1970s who had his own primetime television show. Wilson became popular through his standup routines and comedy albums. Wilson created several popular characters, such as Reverend Leroy, whose hilarious sermons often touched on the realities of black life in the USA more than the sermons of actual preachers did. Another of Wilson's characters was the sassy, showstopping Geraldine Jones. Wilson joined in a common stunt of comedians of that era and dressed in drag.[3] At the time, I was too young to be aware of the implications of Wilson's performing, but I noticed that whenever Geraldine came on the screen, my mother would howl with laughter. My siblings and I rarely saw our mother smiling or laughing, so we were delighted with her elation. One of Geraldine's several catchphrases was "The devil made me do it." In fact, Wilson's fourth comedy album was entitled *The Devil Made Me Buy This Dress*, where he adorned the album cover dressed as Geraldine. Wilson got a generation to laugh over the idea that our outlandish actions are the devil's fault and not our own. Yet all humans must take responsibility for our sins. We also keep in mind that sin is not only indulging in certain vices, like lust, adultery, taking illicit drugs, or cheating on our taxes. Our sin includes whatever attitudes and actions drive a wedge between us and God, or between us and others, or generally hinder the flourishing of God's creation. We must confess our need to be forgiven of all our sins.

Through confession, as part of repentance, we strive to sever our ties with the devil. And in so doing, we become increasingly adept at fighting against injustice and all forms of evil. We learn not to replicate the devil's tactics, which divide, dehumanize, devalue, and destroy. We choose not to hate what God has made. We broadcast truth, bringing clarity to opacity. We radiate light. We know that our struggle is against spiritual forces of evil, so we do not commit violence against other human beings—who are also made in the image of God. Practicing nonviolence is unnatural. In the face of injustice, our human instincts and intuitions push us toward vengeance and retaliation. That is the way of the world, but not the way of Jesus. Jesus came as a human being to earth in order to defeat the works of the devil (1 John 3:8). However, the results of the Lord's victory are yet to be fully realized. The world is still messy. Even so, Jesus fought evil through love, truth, and self-sacrifice. Such behaviors do not appear to be a winning strategy when evil is so prevalent and always appears to have the upper hand. Yet the power of God is evident not only in how Jesus confronted the powers of evil, but in the resurrection. God validated the ministry of Jesus through the resurrection, and one day Satan's defeat will be obvious (1 Corinthians 15:25). It took enormous power for Jesus to fight sin and win, and it will take supernatural power for us to fight like Jesus.

THE BATTLE IS THE LORD'S

My Christian elders would recite a phrase that has appeared in many gospel songs and is meant to be a tonic for weary souls: *The battle is not yours; it's the Lord's!* While the sentence is simple, its message is one of the most difficult lessons to learn. We cannot conceive of what it means for the Lord to fight our battles. We prefer to take matters into our own hands. After all, the way of love feels weak. Non-retaliation appears cowardly. Self-sacrifice seems self-defeating. By contrast, taking revenge provides visceral satisfaction. We are delighted when we learn of victims rising up to mete out physical, violent punishment on their offenders. Watching movies, we cheer when the perpetrators of evil die in a hail of gunfire, have their blood splattered against the wall, or die in some other gruesome fashion. Somehow those moments soothe our need for balancing the scales of what we think is justice. But justice isn't about revenge. Justice isn't giving people whatever punishment we think they deserve. Justice is about restoration. Justice means getting things to be where God intends them to be. Justice involves truth-telling. Justice involves reparations. It is ultimately God's responsibility to dispense punishment. "Beloved, never avenge yourselves, but leave room for the wrath of God; for it is written, 'Vengeance is mine, I will repay, says the Lord'" (Romans 12:19).

The Hebrew Bible, the Tanak—what Christians often call the Old Testament—contains numerous descriptions of violent acts, with some apparently sanctioned by God. In light of Jesus' teachings on love and non-retaliation (e.g., Matthew 5:39, 43), scholars often struggle to explain the violence that God commands Israel to perform (e.g., Deuteronomy 20:17; Judges 21:11; 1 Samuel 15:3).[4] Such analysis is beyond the scope of this book, but it is important to note that Old Testament violence is neither license for vengeance on a personal scale nor sanction for killing on a national scale. We ought not assume that whatever God did through Israel in the Old Testament serves as a command for individuals and nations to conquer and kill. Furthermore, the New Testament is uniform in its denunciation of hatred and vengeance. It takes the power of the Holy Spirit to refrain from violent retribution. For some of us, the civil rights movement provides a pertinent example of a nonviolent response to injustice. But the nonviolent strategy of the movement is often debated or even debased because our country continues to exercise the same bigotry, racism, and overall injustice of that bygone era. If the battle truly is the Lord's, then faith in Jesus is indispensable. We need the entire armor of God, which consists of truth, justice, and the good news of peace, along with faith, salvation, and the word of God (Ephesians 6:13-17). Those who bear the armor must be fortified through prayer (Ephesians 6:18). Spiritual battles require spiritual weapons. "For the weapons of our warfare are not merely human, but they have divine power to destroy strongholds" (2 Corinthians 10:4).

The Berlin Wall came down on November 9, 1989. East and West Germany were no longer separated. The world was treated to footage of exuberant mobs flooding through the checkpoint and chipping away at the wall. It was a historic moment. The Iron Curtain was being torn down and communism seemed doomed. During that time, I was starting a new church in Brooklyn, and also teaching mathematics and science at a private school. Older faculty members, who lived through the Cold War, understood the monumental nature of what was happening. I was invited to the home of a faculty member for a small dinner party, and the topic of religion arose, largely because of curiosity about my pastoral ministry. An atheist colleague commented that when attending church as a child, she witnessed her elders—many of them European immigrants—offering prayers for the dismantling of communism. This colleague considered such prayers naive. She explained to us that God had nothing to do with what we were witnessing in Germany, Russia, and other places, like Czechoslovakia. Political changes, to this teacher, were outside God's purview. On the contrary, we ought not be cynical about the power of God. God hears the prayers of the faithful. While we do not know how or when we'll witness Satan's ultimate demise, we do get occasional glimpses of what the Lord's victory entails.

THE SPIRITUAL POWER OF MARGINALIZED PEOPLE

History has demonstrated that oppressed people best understand what justice can look like. My former colleague witnessed parishioners offering prayers for communism to fall because they likely had been—or knew well—people who suffered under unjust regimes. Suffering has the ability to push the faithful on to greater faithfulness. While the heat of oppression forces some people to melt, it causes others to harden. Amazingly, those who have endured injustice often possess great faith, which produces spiritual depth, providing motivation and insights for all who follow behind these godly people. We must tap into the spiritual power of those who know oppression. We need not pity them for their suffering, or mock any of their limitations derived from their marginalization. Their reliance on the Holy Spirit is to be emulated, never ridiculed.

Nearly twenty years ago, movie director Spike Lee decried the narrative trope which he labeled "the magical Negro." Films employing this storytelling device highlight an African American character with mystical abilities who rescues or otherwise serves the white characters. Movies such as *The Legend of Bagger Vance*, *Ghost*, and *The Green Mile* serve as quintessential examples. More recently, *Harriet*, the biopic of Harriet Tubman, faced similar criticism. There are some who feel that the protagonist's bravery and success at rescuing slaves was depicted as resulting from the messages she received during her trances rather than from her ingenuity. The concern voiced by Spike Lee, as well as others who recognize the magical Negro motif, is that heroic black characters are celebrated and used only for their special abilities. They are typically uneducated and unsophisticated. Furthermore, the magical abilities of the black characters usually serve the needs of the white hero. I share some of the concerns over the "magical Negro" trope. Our society centers whiteness, so it is not surprising that in books and movies, virtuous characters of color often serve as sidekicks or rescuers of white people. These concerns notwithstanding, I do want to acknowledge that from a spiritual perspective, marginalized people are often more spiritually keen than those within mainstream culture. God has given spiritual insight to many people who were deprived of society's advantages. God honors people of low status and operates through people and circumstances that appear foolish in the eyes of those lacking spiritual awareness. "But God chose what is foolish in the world to shame the wise; God chose what is weak in the world to shame the strong" (1 Corinthians 1:27).

We need not create an oversimplified, binary, either-or situation. Marginalized people do not exist to offer white people esoteric, mystical, or magical insights. However, spiritual awareness born of oppression is real. That awareness is useful for everyone, not just white people. Marginalized people are not one-dimensional. We can be spiritually in sync with God and simultaneously well-educated. We have continually demonstrated intelligence, ingenuity, courage, and other virtuous behavior even when white society characterized us as ignorant, savage, lazy, and cowardly. However, suffering does not automatically guarantee spiritual insight. There may be a correlation but not causation. This is to say that suffering provides opportunities for spiritual growth, but we don't always avail ourselves of the lessons. We struggle to alleviate personal problems, and even have theological systems that deny the reality of sickness and pain. Prosperity teachers, for example, emphasize physical wellness and material abundance as signs of God's favor on the faithful. In fact, these teachers consider lack of faith to be responsible for sickness and poverty. However, many followers of Jesus among marginalized people became spiritual giants because they persevered as their faith was tested. As a result, they matured, gaining godly wisdom and insight. Note these opening words of the New Testament letter from James, the brother of the Lord Jesus: "My brothers and sisters, whenever you face trials of any kind, consider it nothing but joy, because you know that the testing of your faith produces endurance; and let endurance have its full effect, so that you may be mature and complete, lacking in nothing" (James 1:2-4). The Holy Spirit works mightily through those who have faithfully endured injustice.

VICTORY FORESHADOWED

Genesis 37–50 relate a saga centering on Joseph, the son of Jacob (whose name was changed to Israel), and Jacob's beloved wife Rachel. This story is too rich with colorful details to recount it all here, but I note a few highlights.

- Young Joseph becomes the object of his ten older brothers' envy because of their father's favoritism. "Now Israel loved Joseph more than any other of his children, because he was the son of his old age; and he had made him a long robe with sleeves. But when his brothers saw that their father loved him more than all his brothers, they hated him, and could not speak peaceably to him" (Genesis 37:3-4).

- Joseph's older brothers consider killing him, but instead sell him into slavery (Genesis 37:18-28). Over many years, Joseph's life takes quite the circuitous route. He's sold to an influential Egyptian, Potiphar, and enjoys a season of success even as a servant (Genesis 39:1-6).

- However, Joseph becomes the victim of sexual harassment and a rape allegation by Potiphar's wife, which sends Joseph to prison (Genesis 39:7-20).

- Because God empowered Joseph with organizational wisdom, along with the ability to interpret dreams, he eventually winds up working for the pharaoh and rising to prominence in Egypt (Genesis 40:1–41:57).

- When a famine hits, Egypt is secure because of Joseph's wisdom in planning, but other areas are devastated. In time, Jacob sends his sons to get grain from Egypt, and, as we readers anticipate, the brothers discover that not only is Joseph alive, but he has power over them (Genesis 45:1-15).

- As the astounding story wraps up, there is an episode in which Joseph's brothers offer themselves as slaves, but Joseph is not interested in retribution. "But Joseph said to them, 'Do not be afraid! Am I in the place of God? Even though you intended to do harm to me, God intended it for good, in order to preserve a numerous people, as he is doing today. So have no fear; I myself will provide for you and your little ones.' In this way he reassured them, speaking kindly to them" (Genesis 50:19-21).

The story of Joseph contains more lessons that we can enumerate, but I want to focus on those that relate to the power of the Spirit. Consider, for example, that Joseph was imprisoned falsely for years before he got an audience with Pharaoh. God's spirit preserved Joseph. Joseph did not know that he would be freed one day, or that he would have an opportunity to confront those who sought to kill him. The timing of justice is unpredictable, but every good thing that happened to Joseph along the way foreshadowed victory. The spirit of God not only preserved Joseph, but enabled Joseph not to take vengeance on his brothers. One thing that Joseph's story communicates is that God is present with those who suffer unjustly. Not every injustice is overturned in our lifetimes, but some are.

Victims of injustice have always challenged God with "How long?" (e.g., Psalm 35:17; Habakkuk 1:2). There are no easy answers to this question. We understand that God is patient and is waiting for people to repent (2 Peter 3:9). We also believe that those who suffer in this life will receive a reward in the life to come: "If we endure, we will also reign with him" (2 Timothy 2:12). Jesus pronounces, "Blessed are those who hunger and thirst for justice, for they will be satisfied" (Matthew 5:6, my translation).[5] However, the timing of that satisfaction is part of the difficulty. It's like the mournful words that Sam Cooke wrote and sang: "It's been a long, long time coming / But I know a change is gonna come."

Our spiritual heroes often came to the sober realization that victory over injustice might never be fully experienced in their lifetimes. Indeed, ultimate justice is reserved for when the Lord returns, as noted in the previous chapter. However, on the road to final redemption we get occasional assurances that "a change is gonna come."

Lawyer and activist Bryan Stevenson's *Just Mercy: A Story of Justice and Redemption* tells the story of the injustices heaped upon Walter McMillian while also painting a picture of various ways the USA's prison system abuses African Americans and other marginalized people. McMillian's story did not play out exactly like Joseph's, but eventually McMillian was released through Stevenson's diligent advocacy. The tenacity of Stevenson, a Christian, as well as the courage of McMillian, shows the power of the Spirit to give a taste of what victory over injustice could be. Stevenson's Equal Justice Initiative continues to work on behalf of victims of injustice, especially people on death row. Sometimes good work in the here and now anticipates what God will ultimately accomplish at the end of time.

Spiritual conversions can foreshadow the victory of God over injustice. However, I stress that conversion is an ongoing process. Conversion through the Holy Spirit is in line with how we defined the gospel in the first chapter. Since the gospel is more than a set of propositions, conversion must be more than intellectual assent to a set of propositions. Since the gospel is not simply a free ticket to heaven, conversion is not merely gracious acceptance of that ticket. The gospel encompasses the story of Jesus—including the teachings and actions of Jesus—and engenders liberation from sin through the death and resurrection of Jesus, and must be embodied within community; conversion involves commitment to all of that. Conversion starts with a commitment to follow Jesus wholeheartedly. Conversion is also an ongoing process because we do not see the entire pathway at the beginning of the journey. By the grace of God, there are countless lives converted by the Holy Spirit, through faith in Jesus Christ. These converts are examples of God's power to subvert the work of the adversary.

During my three decades as an urban pastor, I served two established churches, and also planted two others in major cities. Each congregation sought to some degree or another to be intercultural, intergenerational, and economically diverse. As a result, I've witnessed hundreds of people negotiate the demands of contemporary life while trying to understand the words of Scripture as well as the promptings of the Holy Spirit. I'll not mention names, but in my mind's eye I see individuals who claimed to be followers of Jesus, but through their actions demonstrated greater hope in political outcomes or their bank accounts than in the Spirit of God. They mocked the residents of the neighborhood where the church gathered, rather than finding ways to demonstrate love. Some of the people sought ways to erect larger hurdles to impede those outside the church from becoming part of the church. Fear, rather than faith, undergirded budgetary and other programmatic decisions. They quenched the Holy Spirit, failing to experience power to transform lives and circumstances.

Conversely, I also picture the faces of many who let the power of the Holy Spirit energize their hearts and renew their minds. These converts realized that faith in Jesus meant little if they did not strive "to loose the bonds of injustice" (Isaiah 58:6). The power of the Spirit compelled these disciples of Jesus Christ to move into economically disadvantaged neighborhoods. The power of the Spirit pushed these people to use their education and other resources to fight injustice. The power of the Spirit caused these Christ-followers to find employment wherever they could positively influence the lives of marginalized people most directly. The Spirit empowered these disciples of Jesus to "walk by faith, not by sight" (2 Corinthians 5:7).

Victory over demonic forces does not always make the headlines, as with the fall of the Berlin Wall. However, Satan loses influence in every family that learns how to love more freely and pray more earnestly. Evil is held at bay when our schools get better resources so that children's lives can be enriched. Demonic forces are weakened when more people have access to clean water, affordable housing, healthcare, and safe policing. The Spirit's power isn't reserved for Sunday worship services, and is available to help us tackle injustice.

TEN

The Power of Love

And now faith, hope, and love abide, these three;
and the greatest of these is love.

—1 CORINTHIANS 13:13

WHATEVER LOVE ENTAILS, to some people it includes ignoring the realities of injustice. This seems to be the popular view of love in US Christianity. Popular love shifts the responsibility onto victims, requiring them to forgive while the fate of perpetrators remains ambiguous. Brutalized wives have been told to forgive their abusive husbands. We require victims of racial discrimination to forgive those who have exploited them. This kind of love means handholding, group hugs, and potluck dinners between alienated parties without confronting the underlying causes of that alienation. This perspective of love faults Jews for remembering the Shoah, or African Americans for acknowledging slavery. It requires the ones mentioning racism to apologize for bringing up such a divisive topic. Love without justice claims to seek unity, but in actuality requires uniformity. This love sacrifices truth. Yet we need love. Love is nonnegotiable. Love is the way of Jesus. "Whoever does not love does not know God, for God is love" (1 John 4:8). Dignity is part of true love. Love affirms our personhood. As we forgive those who have sinned against us, we do not jettison truth for the sake of an emotional high. Victims of injustice yearn for better definitions and examples of love.

The verse above (1 Corinthians 13:13) comes from one of the most familiar chapters in the Bible. My years of experience suggest 1 Corinthians 13 is by far the most popular passage read at weddings. Yet the apostle Paul did not seem to have weddings in mind when he wrote these verses. His message was meant to be about more than two people who pledge themselves to each other in marriage. Paul's ode to *agape* is part of his larger project of reconciliation among the Corinthians. The love chapter, 1 Corinthians 13, is an admonition to the fragmented Christian community in Corinth. Factionalism had taken hold (1 Corinthians 1:10-13). It's not hard to imagine groups within those Corinthian gatherings belittling others. Division was evident in various contexts, including the love feast associated with communion.

> When you come together, it is not really to eat the Lord's supper. For when the time comes to eat, each of you goes ahead with your own supper, and one goes hungry and another becomes drunk. What! Do you not have homes to eat and drink in? Or do you show contempt for the church of God and humiliate those who have nothing? What should I say to you? Should I commend you? In this matter I do not commend you! (1 Corinthians 11:20-22)

While Paul offers practical solutions for dealing with problems in Corinth, the main issue was not potluck protocols. Nor

THE POWER OF LOVE / 171

was all division the result of theological disputes, at least not in the way we think of doctrinal differences today. Issues related to honor and status were also behind the Corinthian communion controversy. The remedy for the Corinthians' dysfunction would not start with pious acts of devotion, or with programs designed to make the community more receptive to the notion of unity among the members. The corrective for conflict is love.

Paul ends the chapter with his triad of virtues that appear together elsewhere in his writings: faith, hope, and love (e.g., 1 Thessalonians 1:3; 5:8). He declares that love is the greatest of these noble qualities. Love is the solution to our disunity problem. The key to unity is not found in frequent prayers, increasing church attendance, or performing some heroic act of service. Those actions might be attempts to demonstrate faith in God. Our reading about unity, listening to podcasts about unity, and attending conferences about unity might demonstrate our hope for unity. However, lasting unity is not found in the umpteen Christian conferences offering strategies for less division. While we rightly appeal to faith and hope, we must not bypass love.

SECURE IN GOD'S LOVE

Demonstrating love is nearly impossible for those who have not experienced love. Perhaps many of our societal dysfunctions—including self-centeredness—are the result of a love deficit. The household of my childhood did not communicate or demonstrate love, except in the sense of duty. Love meant fulfilling responsibilities. I can recall only once seeing my parents behave affectionately toward each other. My definitions of love came from television and movies, which is inadequate and artificial. In addition to my homelife, my church experience

presented an angry God who withheld love until we proved ourselves worthy of it. God was not eager to save sinners, but would
do it if the sinner was demonstrably repentant. God preferred
extroverts who could perform their sorrow over sin publicly and
thus show themselves to be worthy of love. Being an introvert,
I seemed destined to never satisfy God's requirements. I spent
years trying to never mess up, hoping that maybe God would
love me. One day while walking to class during my freshmen
year of college, an upperclassman who knew me from the football team passed by, saying, "Dennis walks like a robot." He
smiled and kept going, but I became increasingly self-conscious.
I realized that being afraid of God influenced everything in my
life—even how I physically carried myself. I never wanted to
make a mistake that would upset God. I'm still sorting things
out. My view of God's love was conditional, to say the least.

Even though I heard many sermons and Bible lessons over
the years about God's love, including how God's *agape* is unconditional and given freely, the message found a home in my
head, but not always in my heart. As one friend put it to me,
"You need to know you're loved deep down in your bones!" I
sang what we taught the children:

Yes! Jesus loves me.
Yes! Jesus loves me.
Yes! Jesus loves me.
For the Bible tells me so.

Believing the words of the Bible about Jesus' love is not
the same as experiencing that love for myself. There are many
Scripture passages about God's love and desire to be in fellowship with all of creation. The prophet Jeremiah quotes God

as telling Israel, "I have loved you with an everlasting love" (Jeremiah 31:3). The prophet Hosea had dramatic dealings with an unfaithful wife in order to demonstrate God's love for people who had been spiritually unfaithful. Despite Israel's spiritual adultery, God continually wooed his people, at one point saying through Hosea, "My heart recoils within me; my compassion grows warm and tender" (Hosea 11:8). In the New Testament, the apostle Paul rhetorically asks the Christians in Rome, "If God is for us, who is against us?" (Romans 8:31). Paul follows up his question with affirmations of God's love demonstrated in Jesus the Son, climaxing with this assertion in verses 38-39:

> For I am convinced that neither death, nor life, nor angels, nor rulers, nor things present, nor things to come, nor powers, nor height, nor depth, nor anything else in all creation, will be able to separate us from the love of God in Christ Jesus our Lord.

Of course, reading Bible verses does not guarantee we will experience the love that the verses describe. But meditating on them is a start. God's words of love need to wash over all of us who have felt unloved or unlovable. There is power in letting the positive words of Scripture sink into our subconscious.

The power of love also comes through experience. Earlier I discussed some aspects of worship, and much of worship involves *doing*. Our devotion to God leads us to do things for God. But *being* is at least as important as *doing*, and may actually be of greater value. What I mean by *being* is taking time to be with God so as to be shaped and nurtured by God. It is not rushing to do things for God. In that time of being with God we can start to experience God's unconditional and lavish love.

We can learn that God's love is not contingent on our performance. We can come to see ourselves as worthy of God's love. We also experience God's love by being part of loving communities that see us, know us, and accept us. We become more confident of God's love when we experience it through others. Being secure in God's love paves a way for us to offer God's love to others. Being secure in God's love increases our resilience when facing injustice. Being secure in God's love helps us to love ourselves.

LOVE FOR OURSELVES

The Gospels record Jesus echoing the Old Testament command to "love your neighbor as yourself" (Leviticus 19:18; Matthew 19:19; Mark 12:31). That command reverberates throughout the New Testament (e.g., Romans 13:9; Galatians 5:14; James 2:8). Love for others is predicated on self-love. If we love ourselves well, we have a better sense of what it means to love others. Yet many of us struggle to love ourselves. The demonic powers of racism and whiteness are responsible for part of the struggle some of us have in loving ourselves. For eons, Christians taught that the enslavement of Africans was the result of the so-called "curse of Ham" (Genesis 9:20-27). Part of the religious justification for the transatlantic slave trade was this alleged curse, in which Ham, considered to be the father of Africans, was destined to be a slave to his brothers. As ludicrous as this claim is, it took hold in many sectors of Christianity and persisted.[1] I was taught the curse of Ham in the church of my childhood. Many African Americans grew up with the message not only that God sanctioned slavery, but that there was something inherently wrong with being black. European Christianity, and its offshoot in the New World, has long demonized blackness.

Biblical scholar Gay Byron asserts, "It is clear that assumptions about ethnic and color differences in antiquity influenced the way Christians shaped their stories about the theological, ecclesiological, and political developments within the early Christian communities. As a result, Egyptians, Ethiopians, Blacks, and blackness invariably became associated with the threats and dangers that could potentially destroy the development of a certain 'orthodox' brand of Christianity."[2] *Black* became synonymous with *evil*, and the association remains with us still. For example, evangelical gospel presentations include *The Wordless Book* (and its innumerable variations that are not books, but objects such as bracelets and jelly beans), in which colors are used to lead children to conversion. *Red* represents the blood of Jesus, but *black* represents sinful humans. *White*, of course, represents what is holy and pure: God, as well as the new life after conversion. *Black* is to be avoided; *white* is desirable and necessary. Such presentations of the gospel contribute to an understanding that everything black—including skin—is inherently evil. God saves people, but God doesn't change our skin color. Indeed, our ethnic identity, including racial distinctions, carry over into the afterlife (Revelation 7:9).

The racism within Christianity reflects the white supremacy of the larger society. People of color continually receive messages—overtly as well as subliminally—that we are not worthy of love. We may be worthy of pity, but not love. Recently, I was teaching a biblical theology of race and ethnicity in a doctor of ministry course, and was surprised to find that several of the white students had never heard of psychologists Kenneth and Mamie Clark. The Clarks' story is a remarkable one, considering how rare it was for African Americans to obtain doctoral degrees in the early twentieth century. Perhaps what is most famous about the Clarks is their doll experiment, the results of which were instrumental in desegregating schools in the USA. Thurgood Marshall used the Clarks' data in arguing before the Supreme Court in the famous *Brown v. Board of Education* case of 1954. While the doll experiment has had its critics over the years, there have also been those who built on the Clarks' research. In the original experiment, as well as in some of the re-creations in later years, African American and white children generally preferred white dolls, perceiving them as better than black dolls. The children viewed black dolls as ugly and bad, reflecting how they saw themselves. Whiteness impacts people's self-perception.

Clinical psychologist and Christian minister Chanequa Walker-Barnes discusses self-perception in her analysis of the intersection of race and gender: "When people of color internalize the view that whiteness is superior to all other races (including their own), we call this *internalized oppression*."[3] Walker-Barnes goes on to explain, "The internalization of racism often means that people of color devalue our own bodies, our aesthetics, and our cultural and family values, norms, and beliefs. It also means that we tend to pathologize our own cultures, blaming them for anything that we see as a shortcoming in ourselves, our families, or our institutions."[4] The contemporary phrase "Black lives matter" is offered as fuel for our self-love. It is an anti-brutality slogan, but serves to remind us of our inherent worth as human beings. In my era, we needed to hear and echo James Brown: "Say it loud—I'm black and I'm proud!" We needed to say "Black is beautiful" to ourselves and to each other. I have found myself listening to Christina Aguilera sing, "I am beautiful, no matter what they say. / Words can't bring me down." The song has been part of my self-love strategy. We needed to acknowledge our beauty to counter the degrading messages. We need to love ourselves and find power in love.

LOVE IS HONEST

I confess that too many times in my life I yielded to the temptation to keep quiet as a victim of injustice because I was taught that love should overlook the wrong that had been done to me. Perhaps I mistook silence for love. Maybe I assumed that justice should be reserved for the age to come and not matter in this present age. I had been conditioned to accept evil. But love does not mean ignoring evil, or minimizing injustice. Love puts a spotlight on injustice.

Paul's tribute to love in 1 Corinthians 13 includes lofty attributes in verses 4-7.

> Love is patient; love is kind; love is not envious or boastful or arrogant or rude. It does not insist on its own way; it is not irritable or resentful; it does not rejoice in wrongdoing, but rejoices in the truth. It bears all things, believes all things, hopes all things, endures all things.

This paragraph celebrates love's magnificence. Among love's qualities is its ability to rejoice in the truth and not rejoice in wickedness or wrongdoing. Love prefers honesty. Love does not tolerate lies. Love refuses to celebrate sexual abuse, the demonization of immigrants, mocking of differently abled people, or otherwise communicating disdain for humans—all actions that many in our country have tolerated or even endorsed. Love cannot turn a blind eye to injustice. Love cannot flourish when facts are withheld. Love doesn't cry "Fake news!" when faced with uncomfortable information. Love requires honesty. Theologian Miroslav Volf writes of the moral obligation to remember truthfully in the quest for justice and movement toward unity. "So the obligation to truthfulness in remembering is at its root an obligation to do justice, even in such a seemingly simple act as the 'naming' of what one person has done to another."[5]

Of course, forgiveness is an aspect of love, and people of color are often told that we need to forgive injustice. Forgiveness is taken by some to mean the forgetting of wrongdoing. Some high-profile examples of African Americans forgiving killers may have contributed to an expectation that we will ignore the impact of evil in a rush to forgive. Indeed, we have so often demonstrated forbearance and willingness to forgive the sins of oppressors. In 2015, young white supremacist Dylann Roof was welcomed into the midweek prayer meeting of Mother Emanuel AME Church in Charleston, South Carolina. Roof opened fire on the attendees, killing nine people, including the senior pastor of the congregation, Rev. Clementa Pinckney. Some members of the church went on to offer forgiveness to the killer. Unfortunately, the grace of forgiveness is exploited by some to obfuscate injustice. Jennifer Berry Hawes, a Pulitzer Prize–winning reporter, wrote a book about the massacre at Mother Emanuel. In an interview she discussed the impact of some members of the church forgiving Roof. "There were those who felt strongly that the narrative, while beautiful and inspiring, also took some of the wind from the sails of really pressing for meaningful changes that would address racism and racial disparities."[6]

In 2018, Amber Guyger, a Dallas police officer, shot and killed an unarmed black man, Botham Jean, in his own apartment. Guyger claimed she had mistaken Jean's apartment for her own and thought her neighbor was an intruder. Guyger was found guilty of murder in the fall of 2019. What amazed and confounded many, however, was how the victim's brother, Brandt Jean, forgave Guyger, even hugging her in the courtroom. Brandt Jean said he "needed to be free from the burden of unforgiveness."[7] Indeed, unforgiveness can be a burden. Howard Thurman observed, "Love is possible only between two freed spirits."[8] We follow the command of Jesus: "Love your enemies" (Matthew 5:44). However, our desire to forgive does not ignore or minimize the urgency of truth and justice. We work to free ourselves from hatred while God works on the privileged to free them from their need to control people, information, and outcomes.

LOVE PURSUES JUSTICE

Promise Keepers is a national movement "focused on helping men live with integrity," according to their website. A few years before the movement started, I served a church under the pastor who led the racial reconciliation component of Promise Keepers. Being part of mainstream evangelicalism, Promise Keepers was naturally overwhelmingly white, but the leadership expressed a desire to build bridges between different racial groups. During the 1990s, Promise Keepers reached its apex, holding events in stadiums around the country. After a good friend of mine attended one of the stadium events, he mentioned his frustration at what happened during the challenge for racial reconciliation. In addition to prayer, there had been an invitation for men to hug someone of another race. My friend received a good deal of attention from tearful white attendees who were moved by the speaker's presentation. Yet my friend balked when someone tried to hug him. He told his bleacher neighbor that it's easy to hug in a stadium. Hugging at an emotional moment is not reconciliation. My friend challenged the white fellow attendee to find an African American neighbor in his own community with whom he could form a relationship. What my friend and I were seeing in Promise Keepers, even if they did not intend it, was consistent with evangelicalism's persistent tendency to minimize the painful truths of racism for a warm moment of apparent unity.

The term *racial reconciliation* was popular in evangelicalism for quite some time, but does not always prove to be robust enough to handle difficult truths about power, privilege, and governmental policies of the past. People of color know that the concept of racial reconciliation runs the risk of masking white supremacy. The term might even stall the process of developing unity. Racial reconciliation echoes the notion of colorblindness, a myth that disrespects the perspectives of marginalized people of color. Colorblind thinking fails to recognize and celebrate the uniqueness of ethnic minorities, and ignores what we've accomplished while enduring adversity and oppression. Equality before God and fellowship in the church does not mean erasing differences; it means embracing them. Disregarding race and ethnicity will not create harmony, nor will it respect the human mosaic that God created. Rather than *racial reconciliation*, I prefer the term *racial justice*, because *justice* suggests truth-telling. Professors and activists Allan Aubrey Boesak and Curtiss Paul DeYoung examine their South African and US contexts, respectively, and denounce the weak application of *reconciliation* present in many Christian contexts.

Far too many initiatives for reconciliation and social justice stop short of completing the work required. In our work and engagement with reconciliation, we have discovered how often reconciliation is used merely to reach some political accommodation that did not address the critical questions of justice, equality, and dignity that are so prominent in the biblical understanding of reconciliation. Such political arrangements invariably favor the rich and powerful but deprive the powerless of justice and dignity. Yet more often than not, this "reconciliation" is presented as if it does respond to the needs for genuine reconciliation and employs a language that sounds like the truth but is, in fact, deceitful.[9]

Racial reconciliation has often ignored issues of justice. Hiring worship leaders or other staff members of color does not make white churches or other Christian organizations racially healthy. Adding women to an organization does not make it immune to sexism. Tokenism isn't justice. Tokenism might help an organization look appealing to outsiders, but does not reflect love. Love pursues justice.

LOVE IS PATIENT

I'd been taught that racism was a bigotry problem. This is to say that racism was about prejudice against people who are different. As a child of the 1970s, I watched the Norman Lear television shows, such as *All in the Family*, *The Jeffersons*, *Sanford and Son*, and *Good Times*, along with the numerous and random television movies that consistently framed America's race problem as one of personal prejudice. From the halls of Congress to the hippies on the corner, the message was that "what the world needs now is love, sweet love," as the popular song admonished. But the love advocated during my wonder years was a sappy sentimentality, not a radical reorientation of priorities. However, love does rearrange our priorities. Love pushes the privileged to relinquish power and compels victims to see beyond the injustice.

I struggle to offer a definition of love, or to give a list of all the practical ways to demonstrate love in an unjust world. Love is chameleon-like; its appearance varies depending on the surroundings. First Corinthians 13 does, however, give us the timeless and ubiquitous character of love. Love's character allows us to patiently travel the path toward genuine reconciliation. Miroslav Volf addresses the interaction of honesty, forgiveness, and injustice, describing the journey that true reconciliation takes.

> As to the *journey*, it follows the path that starts with remembering truthfully, condemning wrong deeds, healing inner wounds, releasing wrongdoers from punishment and guilt, repentance by and transformation of wrongdoers, and reconciliation between the wronged and their wrongdoers; and it ends with the letting go of the memory of wrongdoing. We take this journey partially and provisionally here and now when we forgive and reconcile—and on rare occasions release the memory of wrong suffered. We undertake it once again, definitively and finally, at the threshold of the world to come.[10]

To Volf, "releasing" or letting go of the memory of wrongdoing is not amnesia. It is a "divine gift" that "grows out of a healed relationship between the wrongdoer and the wronged in a transformed social environment."[11]

That transformed environment is the result of the work of justice. Love strives for justice. The ultimate transformed environment will be evident at the consummation of all things, when the Lord Jesus returns. In the meantime, we love with perseverance and patience. As followers of Jesus, our highest aim is to follow the Lord with our whole hearts. In doing so, we will love in word and deed. Our love models God's love. We love because God loves us first (1 John 4:19). Our love demonstrates the nearness of God's kingdom. Our love is tenacious. Our love is patient. Our love is strong enough to fight injustice until Jesus comes again.

Epilogue

I **HAVE OFTEN PREACHED** and taught in predominately black spaces. I have also preached and taught in predominately white contexts as well as in multiracial and multiethnic ones. In those latter spaces I have felt pressure to end my presentations in a way that does not anger or offend white people. Everyone loves a happy ending. We all want to believe that Christians will identify and combat injustice. I believe that people of color do not owe white people a happy ending. It is not our task to monitor or protect white people's feelings. Offending people isn't the goal, but truth can hurt. We don't wait for white people to *get it*, to *get woke*, or to give us permission to do exegesis, to write theologies, or to speak our minds in any arena. We may be on the margins, but we have power from God to change the way Christianity operates.

MOVING FORWARD

After I'd served for about two years as the associate pastor of the DC church that I mentioned at the start of this book, the senior pastor announced his resignation. Some discussion ensued among the leaders as to what my role should be. Some leaders advocated for me to become the next senior pastor. A young man within the church, well respected by many of the white members, took me to lunch around this time. It turned out he wanted to discuss my future at the church. He went on to inform me that as he saw it, I had three options: (1) I could leave; (2) I could stay at the church but not preach about "racial reconciliation"; or (3) I could stay and preach about reconciliation, but needed to realize there would be "carnage." I can never forget that last word because it struck me as an especially graphic way to picture church relationships. Carnage suggests war, and with war there are only losers. There are also plenty of casualties in war. As this young man spoke to me, I wondered why I should entertain any of his thoughts concerning my professional future. He seemed to prefer the first option, that I would leave. But who was this person to tell me what my options were?

My temperament and experience at that point caused me to be concerned that many others in the church felt the way this young man did. Perhaps he was their emissary, sent to confront me on their behalf. That young man was demonstrating how power often operates in white-dominated spaces. *Whiteness* is a demonic force, exerting power over people of color. Some white people, especially men, have a tendency to try to put people of color in our place. And our place is rarely a position of leadership over them. Over the next few years, it became increasingly clear to me that even though many whites in that church were comfortable—and even excited—about my pastoral leadership, and the numbers of attendees was increasing, there were influential white people who did not want me as their pastor. My race was a factor. The refrain that came back to me from the influential suburban members was that "Dennis is concerned about city people; there'll be no place for us." Somehow church ministry had become a zero-sum game in their minds. I resigned not knowing what would be next.

One of my African American friends, to whom I recounted some of my painful experiences within white evangelicalism, once said to me, "Dennis, you need to say, 'Father forgive them, for they know not what they do,' and move on." She did well to have given me the words of Jesus from the cross in Luke 23:34. I needed to forgive, but in the way that Miroslav Volf describes—releasing my burden without having amnesia about being wronged. In releasing my burden, I became even freer to serve the Lord without compromising my racial identity.

BRINGING OUR VOICES TOGETHER

One of my hopes is to see more collaboration among people of color. While we often get invited—one or a few at a time—to speak or otherwise participate at white conferences or institutions, there is ongoing need for us to come together apart from a white organization's agenda. Such gatherings are happening and must continue. Sometimes white institutions hire us, but just one of us in a particular discipline. More than one of us at a time might communicate too dramatic of a shift for their white constituents to handle. Consequently, we struggle alone in Christian institutions, or with few associates of color. At the same time, we may be expected to bring changes to the institution—but not too many and none that actually shift the power dynamics. We may be expected to teach with excellence, while also being assigned to boards and committees because more diversity is needed in those groups. We may be asked to represent our institution in other spaces, but not ruffle any feathers. And in all this, we must keep ourselves connected to our own people.

After all, we do not want to lose the prophetic perspective that marginalized people have because we've become part of a white institution. Marginalized people have always had to *code-switch*, being expert at maneuvering in multiple worlds. That expertise is another superpower for us to use in service to the Lord.

ALWAYS BEING WATCHED

I've pointed out that many people of color are used to being eyed with suspicion in certain white contexts—even Christian ones. We may have gotten so used to it that we don't really notice it anymore. I figure that since white people are watching us, we will continue to demonstrate a robust commitment to Jesus and his gospel that might bring some needed changes to the practice of Christianity in the USA. Biblical scholar Lisa Bowens writes about African American perspectives on the apostle Paul from various interpreters throughout our history. One of her conclusions is that

> for far too long the burden for racial justice has fallen upon African Americans, who have marched, protested, written books, signed petitions, given presentations, preached, prayed, sang songs, and even died in the quest for equality. Thankfully many white Christians have been part of this struggle as well, but too many still do not see racism as a problem or not their problem. These early [African American] interpreters urge white believers in their time and in ours to answer the call for justice by sharing the burden of their sisters and brothers of color.[1]

As white folks watch us, some will join in the struggle.

It's like another scene from *Black Panther*. Near the end of the film, when King T'Challa and his compatriots address the United Nations, the king says that Wakanda will finally be sharing their knowledge, resources, and commitment to unity with the outside world. He concludes with the heartwarming line: "We must find a way to look after one another as if we were one single tribe." A question then arises from a white listener: "With all due respect, what can a nation of farmers offer the rest of the world?" Moviegoers smile because we know how awesome Wakanda and its people are. In our real world, we might be dismissed—even respectfully—by some, but we are more awesome than many realize. Marginalized people have a way of being Christian that is meaningful for the entire world and can help us live in unity, even though we are wonderfully different.

KEEP LOOKING TO JESUS

In this book I sought to rightly explain parts of Scripture without being overly technical. Scripture study, along with experience, framed my presentation, with the goal of encouraging all marginalized Christian people to follow Jesus boldly, even if that looks different from white Christianity in the USA. Of course, I did not touch on everything. There is much more that can be said about power, privilege, and Christian faith. Those lessons must keep coming. Sometimes the words will be fiery, sometimes conciliatory, but hopefully they will always be Jesus-centered.

Followers of Jesus always face opposition. The opposition is primarily about our commitment to Jesus in a world that resists our Lord, but is compounded by race, gender, physical ability, education, income, and so many other factors. Yet our Lord says, "In the world you face persecution. But take courage; I have conquered the world!" (John 16:33). Let's keep taking courage by looking to the conquering King. He has given us the power we need to fight injustice until he returns.

Notes

Introduction

1   While I understand that *America* is often used as a synonym of *USA*, I have chosen not to use it as such in this book. I use the abbreviation *USA* (or *US*) when discussing Christianity in my country because I do not feel equipped to address Canadian, Central American, or South American contexts, which could reasonably fall within the descriptor *American* (*America*, however, refers to the USA in some quotations throughout the book).

2   Robin J. DiAngelo, *White Fragility: Why It's So Hard for White People to Talk about Racism* (Boston: Beacon Press, 2018), 43.

3   DiAngelo, *White Fragility*, 43. Italics in the original.

4   DiAngelo, *White Fragility*, 43.

5   Howard Thurman, *Jesus and the Disinherited* (Boston: Beacon Press, 1996), 3. First published by Abingdon Press in 1949.

Chapter 1: The Power of God

1   Lisa Sharon Harper, *The Very Good Gospel: How Everything Wrong Can Be Made Right* (Colorado Springs: WaterBrook, 2016), 14.

2   Frederick Douglass, *Life of an American Slave* (Boston: Anti-Slavery Office, 1845), http://utc.iath.virginia.edu/abolitn/abaufda14t.html. Emphasis in the original.

3   Shannon Van Sant, "'There Is Clearly Something Happening': Fires Destroy 3 Black Churches In Louisiana," NPR, April 6, 2019, https://www.npr.org/2019/04/06/710711294/there-is-clearly-something-happening-3-black-churches-are-set-on-fire-in-louisia.

4   Martin Luther King Jr., "Letter from Birmingham Jail," in *Why We Can't Wait* (Boston: Beacon Press, 1963), 95–96.

5   Matthew W. Bates, *Salvation by Allegiance Alone: Rethinking Faith, Works, and the Gospel of Jesus the King* (Grand Rapids: Baker Academic, 2017), 30. Emphasis in the original.

6   See Magnus Zetterholm, *Approaches to Paul: A Student's Guide to Recent Scholarship* (Minneapolis: Fortress Press, 2009), 62–63.

7   Howard Thurman, *Jesus and the Disinherited* (Boston: Beacon Press, 1996), 4–5.

8   Thurman, *Jesus and the Disinherited*, 5–6.

9   Michael J. Gorman, *Becoming the Gospel: Paul, Participation, and Mission*, The Gospel and Our Culture Series (Grand Rapids: Eerdmans, 2015), 216.

10   Craig S. Keener, *Acts: An Exegetical Commentary*, vol. 1 (Grand Rapids: Baker Academic, 2012), 381.

Chapter 2: The Power of Diaspora People

1   Howard Thurman, *Jesus and the Disinherited* (Boston: Beacon Press, 1996), 12.

2   Thurman, *Jesus and the Disinherited*, 18.

3   Jonathan Walton, *Twelve Lies That Hold America Captive: And the Truth That Sets Us Free* (Westmont, IL: InterVarsity Press, 2018), 7, 17–25.

4   Walton, *Twelve Lies*, 18.

5   Willie James Jennings, *Acts: A Theological Commentary on the Bible* (Louisville: Westminster John Knox, 2017), 6. Emphasis in the original.

6   Albert J. Raboteau, "American Salvation: The Place of Christianity in Public Life," *Boston Review* 30, no. 2 (April 2005): 6.

7   Soong-Chan Rah, *The Next Evangelicalism: Releasing the Church from Western Cultural Captivity* (Downers Grove, IL: IVP Books, 2009), 167.

8   Rah, *The Next Evangelicalism*, 188.

9   Heather Thompson Day, "Evangelicals Are Less Likely to Welcome Refugees Than Non-Believers. How Did We Sink So Low?," *Newsweek*, July 11, 2019, https://www.newsweek.com/christians-acceptance-refugees-evangelicals-1448757.

10   Thurman, *Jesus and the Disinherited*, 15–18.

11   John Lewis with Michael D'Orso, *Walking with the Wind: A Memoir of the Movement* (San Diego: Harcourt Brace, 1999), 344–45.

Chapter 3: The Power to Discern Injustice

1   Howard Thurman, *Jesus and the Disinherited* (Boston: Beacon Press, 1996), 3.

2   See the detailed treatment of Christian missionary efforts and perceptions of Africans in Willie James Jennings, *The Christian Imagination: Theology and the Origins of Race* (New Haven: Yale University Press, 2010), 15–206.

3   Bruce C. Birch, Walter Brueggemann, Terrence E. Fretheim, and David L. Peterson, *A Theological Introduction to the Old Testament*, 2nd ed. (Nashville: Abingdon, 2005), 100.

4   Barbara E. Reid, "Editor's Introduction to Wisdom Commentary," in Annette Bourland Huizenga, *1–2 Timothy, Titus* (Collegeville, MN: Michael Glazier, 2016), xxxiii.

5   Brian K. Blount, "The Souls of Biblical Folks and the Potential for Meaning," *Journal of Biblical Literature* 138, no. 1 (2019): 6.

6   Michael J. Gorman, "Protestant Biblical Interpretation," in *Scripture and Its Interpretation: A Global, Ecumenical Introduction to the Bible*, ed. Michael J. Gorman, annot. ed. (Grand Rapids: Baker Academic, 2017), 231.

7   Shawn Kelley, *Racializing Jesus: Race, Ideology, and the Formation of Modern Biblical Scholarship*, Biblical Limits (New York: Routledge, 2002), 4–5.

8   Kelley, *Racializing Jesus*, 5. Emphasis in the original.

9   Reid, "Editor's Introduction to Wisdom Commentary," xxiv.

10   See Emerson B. Powery and Rodney S. Sadler Jr., *The Genesis of Liberation: Biblical Interpretation in the Antebellum Narratives of the Enslaved* (Louisville: Westminster John Knox, 2016); and Vincent Winbush, "The Bible and African Americans: An Outline of an Interpretive History," in *Stony the Road We Trod*, ed. Cain Hope Felder (Minneapolis: Fortress Press, 1991), 81–97.

11   James H. Evans Jr., *We Have Been Believers: An African American Systematic Theology*, 2nd ed. (Minneapolis: Fortress Press, 2012), 2.

12   See Dennis R. Edwards, "New Horizons in Hermeneutics and Exegesis," in *The State of New Testament Studies*, ed. Scot McKnight and Nijay Gupta (Grand Rapids: Baker Academic, 2019), 63–82.

13   As of January 2019, over 88 percent of the members of the 116th Congress identified as Christian. See Pew Research Center, "Faith on the Hill," Pew Forum, January 3, 2019, https://www.pewforum.org/2019/01/03/faith-on-the-hill-116/.

14   Paul Kivel, *Uprooting Racism: How White People Can Work for Racial*

Justice (Gabriola Island, BC: New Society Publishers, 2002), 17.

15   Skot Welch and Rick Wilson, *Plantation Jesus: Race, Faith, and a New Way Forward* (Harrisonburg: Herald Press, 2018), 85.

16   Niki Lisa Cole, "The Most Important Words in Emma Watson's Speech Were about Masculinity," ThoughtCo, last updated March 18, 2017, https://www.thoughtco.com/emma-watsons-speech-were-about-masculinity-3026213.

17   Kat Chow, "'Model Minority' Myth Again Used as a Racial Wedge between Asians and Blacks," NPR, April 19, 2017, https://www.npr.org/sections/codeswitch/2017/04/19/524571669/model-minority-myth-again-used-as-a-racial-wedge-between-asians-and-blacks.

Chapter 4: The Power of Prophecy

1   Ellen F. Davis, *Biblical Prophecy: Perspectives for Christian Theology, Discipleship, and Ministry*, Interpretation, Resources for the Use of Scripture in the Church (Louisville: Westminster John Knox, 2014), 3.

2   Davis, *Biblical Prophecy*, 3.

3   Walter Brueggemann, *The Prophetic Imagination*, 2nd ed. (Minneapolis: Fortress Press, 2001), 21.

4   Brueggemann, *Prophetic Imagination*, 23.

5   Brueggemann, *Prophetic Imagination*, 28.

6   Davis, *Biblical Prophecy*, 2.

7   Charles W. Mills, *The Racial Contract* (Ithaca: Cornell University Press, 1997), 109.

8   David W. Blight, *Frederick Douglass: Prophet of Freedom* (New York: Simon and Schuster, 2018).

Chapter 5: The Power of Anger

1   Mark 1:41 might be another example of the anger of Jesus, but there is considerable debate about whether the text should read "moved with pity" or "moved with anger."

2   Willard M. Swartley, *Covenant of Peace: The Missing Peace in New Testament Theology and Ethics* (Grand Rapids: Eerdmans, 2006), 168–69.

3   Mary Beard, *SPQR: A History of Ancient Rome* (New York: Liveright, 2015), 521.

4   Nurith Aizenman, "Deaths from Gun Violence: How the U.S. Compares with the Rest of the World," NPR, November 8, 2018, https://www.npr.org/sections/goatsandsoda/2018/11/09/666209430/deaths-from-gun-violence-how-the-u-s-compares-with-the-rest-of-the-world.

5   Judith T. Moskowitz, "Go Ahead and Feel the Anger—It Will Encourage Social Change," *The Hill*, March 18, 2018, https://thehill .com/opinion/healthcare/378422-go-ahead-and-feel-the-anger-it-will -encourage-social-change.

6   See Ashley D. Farmer, *Remaking Black Power: How Black Women Transformed an Era*, Justice, Power, and Politics (Chapel Hill: University of North Carolina Press, 2017); Rebecca Traister, *Good and Mad: The Revolutionary Power of Women's Anger* (New York: Simon and Schuster, 2018); and Brittney C. Cooper, *Eloquent Rage: A Black Feminist Discovers Her Superpower* (New York: St. Martin's Press, 2018).

7   Erica B. Edwards, "Toward Being Nobody's Darling: A Womanist Reframing of School Climate," in *International Journal of Qualitative Studies in Education* (forthcoming).

8   Erica B. Edwards, "Toward Being Nobody's Darling."

9   James H. Cone, *Said I Wasn't Gonna Tell Nobody: The Making of a Black Theologian* (Maryknoll, NY: Orbis Books, 2018), 109.

Chapter 6: The Power of Solidarity

1   Clarence Hilliard, "Down with the Honky Christ—Up with the Funky Jesus," *Christianity Today* 20, no. 9 (January 30, 1976), https:// www.christianitytoday.com/ct/1976/january-30/down-with-honky -christup-with-funky-jesus.html.

2   Michael O. Emerson and Christian Smith, *Divided by Faith: Evangelical Religion and the Problem of Race in America* (New York: Oxford University Press, 2000), especially 69–91.

3   Emerson and Smith, *Divided by Faith*, 89.

4   Howard Thurman, *Jesus and the Disinherited* (Boston: Beacon Press, 1996), 88–90.

5   Interview transcript available from the Stanford Martin Luther King, Jr. Research and Education Institute at http://okra.stanford.edu/ transcription/document_images/Vol05Scans/17Apr1960_ InterviewonMeetthePress.pdf.

6   Korie L. Edwards, *The Elusive Dream: The Power of Race in Interracial Churches* (New York: Oxford University Press, 2008), 6. Emphasis in the original.

7   Love L. Sechrest, *A Former Jew: Paul and the Dialectics of Race*, LNTS 410 (New York: T & T Clark, 2009), 230.

8   Sechrest, *A Former Jew*, 230.

Chapter 7: The Power of Worship
1   Martin Luther King Jr., "A Knock at Midnight" (sermon, Mt. Zion
Baptist Church, Cincinnati, OH, June 5, 1963), text available at https://
kinginstitute.stanford.edu/king-papers/documents/knock-midnight.
2   Arthur Sutherland, *I Was a Stranger: A Christian Theology of Hospitality* (Nashville: Abingdon Press, 2006), 5.
3   Dennis R. Edwards, *1 Peter*, SGBC (Grand Rapids: Zondervan,
2017), 49.
4   W. E. B. Du Bois, *The Souls of Black Folk: Essays and Sketches*
(Chicago: A. C. McClurg, 1935), 261.
5   Du Bois, *Souls of Black Folk*, 262.
6   James H. Cone, *The Spirituals and the Blues: An Interpretation* (New
York: Seabury Press, 1972), 30–31.
7   Scot McKnight, *Reading Romans Backwards: A Gospel of Peace in the
Midst of Empire* (Waco, TX: Baylor University Press, 2019), 30.

Chapter 8: The Power of Hope
1   Langston Hughes, "Harlem," in *The Collected Works of Langston
Hughes*, ed. Arnold Rampersad (New York: Vintage, 1995), 426. Text
available at https://www.poetryfoundation.org/poems/46548/harlem.
2   Martin Luther King Jr., *A Testament of Hope: The Essential Writings
and Speeches of Martin Luther King Jr.*, ed. James Melvin Washington
(San Francisco: HarperSanFrancisco, 1991), 327.
3   Martin Luther King Jr., "I've Been to the Mountaintop" (address,
Bishop Charles Mason Temple, Memphis, TN, April 3, 1968), text
available at https://kinginstitute.stanford.edu/king-papers/documents/
ive-been-mountaintop-address-delivered-bishop-charles-mason-temple.
4   Sylvia C. Keesmaat and Brian J. Walsh, *Romans Disarmed: Resisting
Empire, Demanding Justice* (Grand Rapids: Brazos Press, 2019), 190.
The authors reference Walter Brueggemann, "Formlessness of Grief,"
in *The Psalms and the Life of Faith*, ed. Patrick D. Miller (Minneapolis:
Fortress Press, 1995), 81.
5   Keesmaat and Walsh, *Romans Disarmed*, 382.
6   John H. Walton, *Job*, NIVAC (Grand Rapids: Zondervan, 2012), 220.
7   Walton, *Job*, 220.
8   Keesmaat and Walsh, *Romans Disarmed*, 382.

Chapter 9: The Power of the Spirit
1   Robin DiAngelo, *White Fragility: Why It's So Hard for White People to
Talk about Racism* (Boston: Beacon Press, 2018), 71–72.

2   For more on Genesis 3 and how the Bible introduces evil and Satan without explaining their origins, see Dennis R. Edwards, *What Is the Bible and How Should We Understand It?* (Harrisonburg: Herald Press, 2019), 19–20; Walter Brueggemann, *Genesis*, Interpretation: A Bible Commentary for Teaching and Preaching (Louisville: Westminster John Knox Press, 2010), 41–44; and Lloyd Pietersen, *Reading the Bible after Christendom* (Harrisonburg, VA: Herald Press, 2012), 106–7.

3   There's too much to be explored here about the impact of black men performing in drag. In public lectures, missiologist Soong-Chan Rah has discussed the tendency of white society to see African American men as either "threats or pets." When black actors or comedians perform in drag, it contributes to removing their "threat" status, thereby calming the fears of white people.

4   Some resources for exploring this topic of violence in the Old Testament include Gregory A. Boyd, *The Crucifixion of the Warrior God: Interpreting the Old Testament's Violent Portraits of God in Light of the Cross* (Minneapolis: Fortress Press, 2017); David T. Lamb, *God Behaving Badly* (Downers Grove, IL: IVP, 2011); Eric A. Seibert, *Disturbing Divine Behavior* (Minneapolis: Fortress Press, 2009); William J. Webb and Gordon K. Oeste, *Bloody, Brutal, and Barbaric? Wrestling with Troubling War Texts* (Downers Grove, IL: IVP, 2019).

5   The word *dikaiosynē* can be translated as "righteousness" or "justice," and the latter seems to fit the context better.

Chapter 10: The Power of Love

1   For more on the curse of Ham, a good place to start is Edwin M. Yamauchi, *Africa and the Bible* (Grand Rapids: Baker Academic, 2004), 19–33.

2   Gay L. Byron, *Symbolic Blackness and Ethnic Difference in Early Christian Literature* (London: Routledge, 2002), 12.

3   Chanequa Walker-Barnes, *I Bring the Voices of My People: A Womanist Vision for Racial Reconciliation*, Prophetic Christianity (Grand Rapids: Eerdmans, 2019), 71.

4   Walker-Barnes, *I Bring the Voices*, 71.

5   Miroslav Volf, *The End of Memory: Remembering Rightly in a Violent World* (Grand Rapids: Eerdmans, 2006), 54.

6   Adelle M. Banks, "Mother Emanuel's Forgiveness Narrative Is 'Complicated,' Says Reporter-Turned-Author," Religion News, June 6, 2019, https://religionnews.com/2019/06/06/mother-emanuels-forgiveness-narrative-is-complicated-says-reporter-turned-author/.

7   David Ki Lee, "Botham Jean's Brother Honored for Embrace of Dallas Officer Convicted in the Killing," NBC, December 3, 2019, https://www.nbcnews.com/news/us-news/botham-jean-s-brother -honored-embrace-dallas-officer-convicted-killing-n1094801.

8   Howard Thurman, *Jesus and the Disinherited* (Boston: Beacon Press, 1996), 91.

9   Allan Aubrey Boesak and Curtiss Paul DeYoung, *Radical Reconciliation: Beyond Political Pietism and Christian Quietism* (Maryknoll, NY: Orbis Books, 2012), 1.

10   Volf, *End of Memory*, 151.

11   Volf, *End of Memory*, 146.

Epilogue

1   Lisa Bowen, "Liberating Paul: African Americans' Use of Paul in Resistance and Protest," in *Practicing with Paul: Reflections on Paul and the Practices of Ministry in Honor of Susan G. Eastman*, ed. Persian Burroughs (Eugene, OR: Cascade Books, 2018), 71.

The Author

DENNIS R. EDWARDS is associate professor of New Testament at North Park Theological Seminary and the author of *What Is the Bible and How Do We Understand It?* in The Jesus Way series and *1 Peter* in the Story of God Bible Commentary series. A sought-after speaker at conferences and universities and a frequent contributor at Missio Alliance, Edwards has served as a church planter in Brooklyn and Washington, DC, and has worked in urban ministry for nearly three decades. He previously taught New Testament at Northern Seminary. Edwards holds degrees from Cornell University, Trinity Evangelical Divinity School, and Catholic University of America, and is ordained in the Evangelical Covenant Church. He and his wife, Susan Steele Edwards, are the parents of four adult children and grandparents of four grandchildren.